A PINCH O

To Deirdre for her beautiful illustrations and
Bill for his enthusiastic wine suggestions.

To Mark and Gary at Ptarmigan for producing
a book from a pile of greasy kitchen notes.

Deirdre Dyson, Malmesbury, Wilts

Bill Baker, Reid Wines, The Mill, Hallatrow, Bristol

1

Published in the United Kingdom
by Ptarmigan Design Publishing & Print Limited.

Ptarmigan House
No 9 The Coda Centre
189 Munster Road
London SW6 6AW

Telephone: 0171-381 5600
Facsimile: 0171-381 4012

ISBN 0 9526380 53

British Library Cataloguing in Publication Data.
A catalogue record for this book is available from the British Library.

CONTENTS

Foreword	*By Bernard Levin*	5
Introduction	*Stephen Ross*	7
The Bare Necessities	*Stocks, Sauces & Pastries*	9
First Courses	*Soups*	23
	Salads	31
	Fish Dishes	43
	Savoury Beginnings	55
Main Courses	*Fish Dishes*	67
	Poultry and Game	79
	Beef and Lamb	93
	Pork and Offal	103
Puddings	*Sweets*	111
Nibbles	*Before and After*	127

BERNARD LEVIN

The Oxford Dictionary of Quotations has no fewer than sixty-five entries about food, but we must surely begin where the Bible begins with these splendid words: "Butter and honey shall he eat, that he may know to refuse the evil, and choose the good."

Fine words, but you would be amazed to know how many people believe eating is nothing but keeping the belly full, how many are not only ignorant of real eating, and (I shudder at the thought) insist that there is no such thing of pleasure to be found in eating. One can go even further; there are people who insist that eating must not be a pleasure. (And as for drinking wine and enjoying it…!)

Strange, is it not? For those who listen to music are not rebuked, nor do those who wander through art galleries find themselves sneered at, and surely a visit to the theatre is not followed by a reprimand. It is all very well to say that we have to eat; that is true, but why can we not take pleasure from a necessity? Some say that it is the memories of awful childhoods ("… you'll finish your porridge if you have to sit there for an hour…") and I think there is some truth in that theory, for I have my own memories of eating the stuff in my boarding-school.

Very well, very well. I know that there are people who get no pleasure from food. I am sorry for them, but I am certainly not going to join them. On the contrary, when I am in one of my favourite restaurants, and I see a fine plate of fine food making its way towards me, it is all I can do to stifle my cries of joy. And anyway, who said I wanted to stifle my cries of joy?

Because, as any sensible person will tell you that eating good food in good surroundings is a pleasure, and a deep and wonderful pleasure at that. And what is more, we do not have to empty our pockets to eat: there are scores of excellent restaurants with modest prices.

But this goes even more deeply. The taste of good food is not just a pleasure, though of course it is, but it is something more significant and more profound. We know that we would die if we did not eat; throughout the years, indeed the centuries, that truth has been intertwined with the pleasure of eating, and that pleasure has gone far deeper than the multifarious tastes offered in the thousands of restaurants.

Now, we mustn't go too far. A wonderful meal is something to remember, but an evening with Beethoven or Shakespeare is something different. Yet there is another glorious answer to that: we can have both. Remember what I said; there are sixty-five entries in the Oxford Dictionary of Quotations referring to eating, and if there are still curmudgions saying "Shucks, it's only food, you know!" Well, even Scrooge came round in the end.

I started with a Biblical quotation. I shall end with another:

"And the people sat down to eat and drink, and rose up to play".

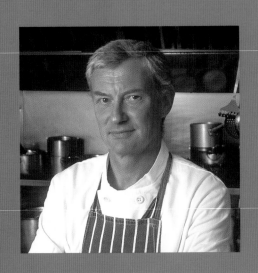

STEPHEN ROSS

A Pinch Of Salt is a light-hearted collection of recipes from our restaurant kitchens; some go back to Popjoys in the seventies, some to Homewood Park in the eighties, but the majority are from The Olive Tree of the nineties. These dishes we have found to be popular, and are all simple to prepare given a modicum of knowledge, enthusiasm and tolerance of some of our culinary idiosyncrasies.

The success of the cookery book industry should have ensured that the entire literate population was incarcerated in their kitchens, putting into practice their newly researched cuisine gleaned from the glossy pages of their most recent purchase. That restaurants thrive must indicate that the seduction of the printed page is only partially successful; as restaurateurs we must encourage that degree of domestic sloth through which we entice our guests to take the easier option and let us do the washing-up. We do provide some atmosphere and service but essentially our gambit is that professional chefs prepare food that is different or beyond the capabilities of the home cook. To demonstrate that this is largely untrue is the purpose of this book; to offer some guidance as to how to make entertaining cookery primarily entertaining for the cook and not an ordeal. If we redistribute a little restaurant caché, all well and good.

There is some satisfaction to be had from the turning full circle of the wheel of culinary fashion; we were introduced to the restaurant business through the kitchens of Kenneth Bell and George Perry-Smith at a time when such gifted amateurs as these were bringing to the drab menus of the sixties the breath of fresh air introduced by writers such as Elizabeth David and Jane Grigson. We have always been more comfortable with a simpler style and watching the trend to over elaborate and poorly crafted food in the country house hotel boom of the eighties was not encouraging. At the top however the Roux brothers, Mosimann, Blanc, Ladenis and others had shown us how to use and nurture fine materials which were becoming increasingly easy to source, and by adopting this approach to simple dishes we have evolved the present style that may be loosely termed the Mediterranean or Brasserie approach. Thus many dishes on today's menu might have appeared twenty-five years ago, but our ingredients are much better and we are more professional in our techniques.

As an informal collection of ideas, we have not attempted text-book guidance to method; the bare necessities chapter provides some assistance with essentials that are needed in the recipes, for the rest we assume some familiarity, or the likely presence at hand of a text by Delia or Roux! Chefs are notoriously vague about cooking times and temperatures; their guide tends to be touch, sight and smell, which actually makes sense, and perhaps one of the pleasures of cookery is making one's own judgements about what seems about right.

Restaurants often have long wine lists but rarely any guidance or linkage to their food; here Bill Baker of Reid Wines has made a wine suggestion for most of the recipes. That all of these suggestions are different demonstrates not only Bill's encyclopaedic knowledge of wine but his huge enthusiasm for cooking and his culinary instinct.

Whatever one may think of these recipes, the watercolours by Deirdre Dyson must be a single delightful reason for turning these pages, and if the adage holds good that it is the pictures that sell cookery books then we shall be set for a future life of ease.

Recipes are rarely single ideas; a kitchen brigade develops, experiments and refines, and a collection of dishes such as these owes much to those with whom we work; thank you for all the help and creative contributions.

Remember to take all the recipes with a pinch of salt!

STEPHEN AND PENNY ROSS 1996

STOCKS, SAUCES & PASTRIES

*W*e had some difficulty in deciding if this section should appear; is it not somewhat impertinent to suggest that a reader may need a recipe for chicken stock? Finally we thought that these essentials may at least save having to heave a massive text book from the shelf, but we have stuck to those methods for fundamentals that are required for these recipes only.

Hopefully this informal small collection of recipes may encourage a few younger cooks to have a go, and by providing a few basic techniques make the book approachable to the inexperienced. I do recall seasoning my first chicken stock with enthusiasm, not realising that it would be later heavily reduced and getting an open-mouthed look of disbelief from the boss, so maybe we are not being too impertinent after all.

Elizabeth David's English Bread and Yeast Cookery runs to 547 pages. Here in somewhat more abbreviated form are two simple bread recipes.

There are endless permutations to bread making; essentially it is the role of the bread in the meal that will determine the style of dough. In a restaurant we are serving bread as an accompaniment to other food and therefore do not want it to be too substantial. At home 'our daily bread' may be a more robust wholemeal, something of a meal in itself.

Wholemeal or wheatmeal flours with little or no extraction of bran produce a heavy dough but are full of flavour and are good for us. The more white flour added the lighter the bread, so a brown bread that is light but with good flavour might be half and half. The white flour should be a strong white which gives a really elastic dough and firm texture; soft flours such as the ordinary plain flour on the supermarket shelf make for a more pappy, cakey texture.

Other choices are the fats and liquids; milk and eggs make for a softer dough, olive oil instead of butter tastes more interesting. Then of course we can put olives in the bread, walnuts, sundried tomatoes, the list is endless.

We use fresh yeast as we use it quickly but dried is fine and keeps better, though not indefinitely. Fresh yeast has that wonderful brewery, malty smell and seems to add to the wholesome process of bread making, which is I suppose why we bother because nowadays there is every variety available to buy.

Allow 2 teaspoons of dried yeast per 1lb (450g) of flour.

OLIVE TREE SOFT WHITE BREAD ROLLS

This will make about 25 small rolls or 2 large loaves:

1½lb (675g) strong white flour

1½lb (675g) soft plain flour

1oz (25g) salt

2oz (50g) caster sugar

2 eggs

2oz (50g) butter

2oz (50g) fresh yeast

1 pint milk

Mix the flours with the salt and stand in a warm place for ½ hour (very low oven will do)

Warm the milk and stir in the yeast and sugar. Stand for ½ hour. Melt the butter.

Work the liquids and eggs into the flour in a food mixer with a dough hook or in a basin by hand until the dough is elastic and cleanly coming away from the sides; more milk may be added if the dough is too dry.

Allow to 'prove' covered with a damp tea towel for about a ½ hour until the dough has doubled in bulk. Knock back, knead thoroughly and for rolls cut into 2oz (50g) bits, roll between the palms, place on a baking sheet and prove again for 15 minutes. Leave room for the rolls to double in size. For loaves, fill tins half full with a nice rounded top or make 'cottage' loaf shapes and place on a baking sheet, proving a little longer than the rolls to double their bulk.

Cook in preheated oven MK 7 220C for 15 minutes for rolls, about 30 minutes for medium loaves. Test by tapping base of loaf which should sound like a taught drum; put loaves back in the oven for a few minutes out of the tins, to form an even crust.

OLIVE TREE BROWN BREAD ROLLS

1½lb (675g) wholemeal flour

1½lb (675g) strong white flour

1oz (25g) salt

3oz (75g) caster sugar

3oz (75g) butter

3oz (75g) olive oil

2oz (50g) fresh yeast

1 pint milk

Proceed exactly as above, adding the oil to the flour with the salt.

This bread is excellent with the addition of some herbs such as basil or rosemary.

STOCKS

Veal, chicken, and fish stocks are the essences of cooking; essential to creating rich flavour and substance, the body that make sauces full of character; sauces made with too much alcohol taste acidic and unbalanced.

When Nico Ladenis, the somewhat intimidating multi-starred chef was looking round my kitchen many years ago, he first asked to see the stock pot; "from this everything else follows" he pronounced and I am sure he was right.

A suggestion is to have a 'stock day' rather like a Monday 'wash day' and make good quantities of stock which can then be frozen in batches.

Don't choose a Monday for the fish stock making because the bones won't be fresh!

CHICKEN STOCK

This is the stock for your pale coloured sauces for poultry or soups.

Put all the ingredients in a large pan, bring to the boil, remove any scum and simmer for 3 to 4 hours, replacing water if necessary. Pass the stock through a fine sieve and allow to cool.

Remove the fat from the top which will have set; put the stock back into the pan and reduce by about half. The stock should now set when chilled.

Ask your butcher for about:
5lb (2K) chicken bones –
very fresh
4 peeled onions
4 carrots
2 sticks celery
A bundle of parsley stalks
8 pints of water

VEAL STOCK

Assemble:

5lb (2k) veal bones from your
friendly butcher (one has to pay
for these bones nowadays)
4 large onions – skins on
4 large carrots
4 sticks celery
A bundle of parsley stalks, thyme
and bay leaves
A little oil for frying
8 pints approx of water
6 tomatoes
2 tablespoons tomato purée

For dark meat sauces. The secret is the reduction to the point that the stock will set to a jelly – proper 'glace de viande'

Roast the bones in a hot oven until well browned and pour away surplus fat.

Sauté the vegetables in the oil until coloured

Put the ingredients with the water in a large pan, bring to the boil.

Remove any scum and simmer for 5-6 hours. Now the crucial bit - chill the strained liquid until the fat has set, remove this from the top and put back on to the stove to reduce until the stock becomes quite dark and sticky to the touch – this is now the basis to your great sauces.

FISH STOCK

3lb (1.4K) fresh fish bones
(avoid oily fish and plaice)
1 peeled onion
2 carrots
1 stick celery
10 peppercorns
5 pints water
¼ bottle white wine
Bundle of parsley stalks

The principle of making fish stock is quite different to that of making meat stock. Only twenty to thirty minutes of simmering is necessary to extract flavour from the bones; longer makes a stock bitter and gluey.

Bring the stock to the boil, remove any scum and after 20-30 minutes sieve carefully and put stock back on heat to reduce by a third for sauce-making. For soup use the stock unreduced.

DRESSINGS

Most restaurants used to have a standard vinaigrette which probably lurked on a shelf above the salad area, never changing, probably rather vinegary. There was olive oil full stop and most chefs knew only one meaning of virgin, and they didn't know many of those!

First the vinegars appeared; sherry, raspberry and balsamic, then all the varieties of oils from hazelnut to truffle, from extra virgin to private reserves. Our bill for oils and vinegars is astonishing but all these goodies have transformed the way we view first courses and salads. Dressings have replaced sauces even for main dishes and it is now common to see warm dressing as sauce for fish or chicken.

It seems to me wasteful to use the finest olive oil to mix with vinegar, so we keep these oils to use on their own.

A blender makes an emulsified dressing which holds on the salad leaves better.

The nutty oils are very strong and walnut and hazelnut are best diluted with a little olive oil, but then used without vinegar, just a little seasoning.

Balsamic vinegar is so concentrated that a very small amount on grilled tuna or salmon is wonderful, just on its own.

For a vinaigrette one might use:
6 parts good olive oil
1 part white wine vinegar
Sea salt, pepper
A little Dijon mustard

A dressing for, say, a chicken liver salad may be more assertive, perhaps:
4 parts olive oil
2 parts sherry vinegar
Finely chopped shallot
Mustard and seasoning

We have experimented with a few relishes; try finely chopped tomato with leek or fennel steeped in 2 parts hazelnut oil, 1 part balsamic vinegar, a little garlic and seasoning with chopped flat leaved parsley. This makes a lovely piquant garnish for grilled chicken or fish.

Hot chilli dressing is one we have made for chargrilled monkfish. Mix a very finely chopped chilli with a little garlic, three skinned and seeded tomatoes, fresh chives, lemon juice, and enough olive oil to make a sauce. Season well.

In summer when looking for a cooler, blander dressing for a cold dish, a yoghurt based dressing is really fresh. Add to some Greek yoghurt, lemon, a little garlic, fresh mint, chives and some finely chopped cucumber or tomato and one has something close to the Greek tzatsiki. With fresh coriander added you have a fine foil for a spicey Indian dish.

SALSA

For salsa verde try this:

12 tablespoons olive oil

Rind and juice of 1 lemon

1 clove garlic

Chopped capers, anchovy and gherkin (about a tablespoon of each)

4 tablespoons chopped parsley

2 tablespoons chopped basil

Salt and pepper

No chef of the nineties can escape without reference to salsa in all its guises, but it is hardly new. Salsa verde should be finely chopped not blended which makes for a green sludge.

Chop small and mix thoroughly. More oil and lemon may be added to make more of a sauce, less of a relish.

Real mayonnaise has been surplanted in most households by that bland, white vegetable fat that dares to call itself real mayonnaise but is not. There is no substitute for the pure emulsion of olive oil, egg yolk, vinegar and lemon juice that is the rich-scented proper mayonnaise, the inspiration for the derivatives of sauce tartare, remoulade et al (twenty in Larousse Gastronomique)

If one is concerned about Edwina Curry's raw egg warnings, ensure that your mayonnaise is quite acidic which is the best protection against bugs.

A few tips – use eggs and oil that are about the same temperature. A little dried English mustard helps the emulsion. Start adding the oil very slowly and if the sauce looks too thick add a dash of boiling water or lemon juice. If disaster strikes fear not and begin again with new egg yolks, adding the curdled sauce as though it was the oil. Be dominant and get on with it, as the sauce may sense your trepidation!

Our staff are tired of my boast that I have never curdled a mayonnaise but it's true!

In a processor or mixer beat the yolks until pale with the lemon, mustard and seasoning. Add the oil first in very small drops, then in a stream. Add the vinegar half way through and finish with the boiling water. The sauce should very thick and a little piquant.

For ½ pint mayonnaise:

3 egg yolks

2 tablespoons lemon juice

1 teaspoon mustard powder

¼ pint olive oil mixed with

¼ pint groundnut oil

1 tablespoon white wine vinegar

seasoning

A dash of boiling water

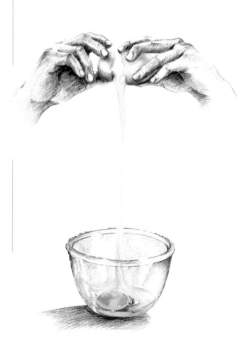

8 portions:

3 egg yolks

Coffeespoon Dijon mustard

Coffeespoon salt

White pepper

2 tablespoons lemon juice

1 tablespoon white wine vinegar

10oz (250g) unsalted butter

A lady once confided to me that she had mastered the art of hollandaise, and that the secret was to put the finished sauce in the airing cupboard, from where just prior to guests sitting down she could hurry down to the kitchen and serve the sauce; I sometimes wondered if the odd sock had ever graced her hollandaise! No mystery surrounds this sauce; avoid getting the sauce too hot or cold, and if the catastrophe happens and it separates, just begin with some new yolks and add the separated sauce as though it was the melted butter. In emergencies I have rescued a sauce by adding the separated sauce to hot double cream!

This sauce can be a base for others; sorrel with the addition of fresh sorrel, sauce choron with tomato or, of course, a Béarnaise with a little more acidity and the addition of fresh tarragon and parsley.

Put all the ingredients except the butter into a basin over a pan of simmering water. Melt the butter in a separate pan. Whisk the egg mixture and bring slowly up to hot but not boiling heat. When hot add the butter in a steady stream whisking vigorously. Do not allow the mixture to get too hot. Add a little hot water if the sauce is too thick. If the sauce begins to look unstable as if about to separate by not clinging to the sides of the bowl, add a little cold water. Adjust the seasoning, and keep hot still in the 'bain-marie'.

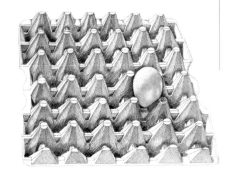

SUGAR SYRUP

Useful for sorbets, meringue Italienne, or even just for fruit salad.

In a very clean and completely dry pan bring 4oz caster sugar to the boil with ½ pint water and simmer to form a light syrup. Further boiling will produce a caramel for a caramel sauce or for 'pulling' sugar strands.

Don't stick your fingers in to taste it!

SHORT PASTRY

The blender allow us to make pastry so quickly and with such confidence that there is little need, especially for short pastry, to resort to the bought variety. The resting of the pastry after making, and the resting of the rolled-out pastry helps greatly to prevent shrinkage.

You need:
12oz (350g) sifted plain flour
Pinch of salt
8oz (225g) butter
2 eggs
Tablespoon of cold water

An all-purpose pastry which with the addition of 2oz (50g) of caster sugar becomes a sweet shortcrust or pâte sablé.

In the blender bring the flour and butter to the 'breadcrumb' stage. Add the whole eggs and water and lightly work together. Allow to rest in the fridge before using. You may need more or less water depending on the size of the eggs.

8oz (225g) butter

8oz (225g) strong white flour

Pinch of salt

3 fl oz cold water

Squeeze of lemon juice

Why make puff pastry when it may be bought at the supermarket? If one is the kind of cook that prepares food from necessity rather than for, sometimes, pleasure then buy puff pastry from the supermarket. If one cooks with a degree of satisfaction at getting something just right then have a go at puff pastry because it is very rewarding, and of course bought puff pastry does not normally contain the pure butter and lack of preservatives of the home-made.

Let your butter reach room temperature. Sift the flour and salt into a basin (or use a blender), add water and lemon juice to make a dough. Rest for 20 minutes (the dough not the cook)

Roll out the dough to a rectangle about ½" thick. Flatten the butter with rolling pin between sheets of greaseproof paper, so that the butter is ⅔ length of the paste and just less than the width. Place the butter at one end of the paste. Fold the flap of paste uncovered by the butter back over the butter. Now fold the flap of paste over again so it completely encases the butter. The effect is of a flattened swiss roll. Place the end of the roll towards you. Roll out to its original size. Fold in three again. Rest for 10 minutes, repeat 5 times. Each rolling is called a turn because the folded paste turns through 90˚ each time, for the end of the roll to be facing you.

PASTRY CREAM – CREME PATISSIERE

The base for those marvellous fruit tarts, filling of choux buns etc. Easy to make, with no alarms about boiling, as the flour prevents the sauce scrambling.

Beat together the yolks, flour and sugar. Pour on heated milk whisking well. Place back in pan and bring to boil, stir until thickened. Allow to cool. Keeps well in the fridge and can be flavoured with rum etc. for fillings – try rum and orange pancakes.

You need:
½ pint milk
2 egg yolks
2 oz (50g) plain flour
1 oz (25g) caster sugar

PROPER EGG CUSTARD

Lovely with spotted dick, but also an excellent base for sweet sauces with the addition of liquer, cream, fruit purée etc. Also essential for the making of ice creams. Chefs refer to this simple confection as 'Anglaise', short for crème Anglaise, a habit I find particularly irritating; custard sounds much more comfortable.

Put the milk into a pan and bring to the boil. Beat the egg yolks, sugar and vanilla in a basin until light and creamy. When the milk is nearly boiling pour onto the egg mixture whisking vigorously. Return the mixture to the pan and on a low heat, stir continuously until thickening enough to coat the back of a wooden spoon. Do not allow to boil. If it begins to scramble don't panic but put the mixture back into the basin you used for the eggs and whisk furiously and with luck you will be saved. Sieve and store if needed with greaseproof paper on the top.

If cream is used with 2 extra yolks you get the classic base for crême brûlée. You will also need it for my bread and butter pudding!

You need
1 pint milk
4 egg yolks
2 oz (50g) caster sugar
Few drops vanilla essence

2lb (1Kg) soft white flour

4oz (110g) caster sugar

8 eggs

½ pint milk

12oz (350g) softened butter

Level tablespoon salt

3oz (75g) fresh yeast

Brioche is that wonderful cross between bread and cake that is so good for breakfast as a change from greasy croissants.

This recipe also provides the yeast pastry, by halving the milk quantity, for the salmon coulibiac (see page 70).

Brioche freezes very well when cooked, so this 4lb quantity is well worth making at once.

Dissolve the yeast in the warm milk. Mix the sugar and flour thoroughly with the salt. Add the beaten eggs and milk to form a light dough. Dot the softened butter in pieces on the top and prove, as for bread, in a warm place for about 30 minutes. Knock back the risen dough and either put into loaf tins, well buttered and half-filled, or into individual brioche moulds.

Allow to prove for a second time. Bake in a medium to hot oven Mk 5 190C for about 30 minutes but check carefully that the top is not burning and reduce heat accordingly. Small brioche moulds will only take about 15 minutes.

SOUPS

"Thank God for soups. They make us money. Every bowl sold boosts the food percentage, water is a profitable ingredient". So it may seem but the reality of course is that we chefs don't think like that, although the banks think that we should. The fact is that soups are one of the most popular restaurant dishes, maybe not as fashionable as in the past because their presentation gives little opportunity for the poseur, but they still remain bedrock good restaurant fare. The commercial kitchen has an advantage in having stocks at hand, but a little forethought and the freezer can make soup-making at home, armed with magimix and liquidiser, very simple. (See Bare Necessities for stocks). Soups express a kitchen's character; British chefs make great winter and vegetable soups, Mediterranean chefs aromatic and fish soups, Americans chowders, and vichyssoise was a New York dish. (Smooth, rich and with simple ingredients?).

So make your soups robust, don't worry about the texture, make good stocks, and think of soup through the seasons; spiced parsnip in January, a heady gaspacho in high summer, fish soup when holidaying by the sea. A soupe au pistou from Provence in cool September, the basil the last of the aroma of summer, and a reminder of colder days ahead.

AVGOLEMENO

One of my favourites – very light, refreshing and great as a cold summer soup with some cream added. If you have your chicken stock all prepared (See Bare Necessities) this is very simple to make but rather impressive for summer entertaining. Take care not to boil the soup when reheating. I have always assumed this to be a Greek soup, although I have never come across it in Greece, but Elizabeth David refers to it as a Greek soup so I am certainly not going to disagree!

Cook the rice in the seasoned chicken stock with the parsley stalks. (20 minutes) Beat the egg yolks with the lemon juice, grated rind and finely chopped parsley. When ready to serve, ensure the stock is off the boil, pour onto egg mixture, whisking vigorously.

Serve immediately, with fresh chopped parsley.

To reheat do not allow to boil.

If serving cold, add ¼ pint double cream, and sprinkle with chopped chives.

A more substantial broth can be made by adding diced pieces of chicken breast to poach in the stock for five minutes.

You will need for 8 generous portions:

3 pints chicken stock

1 pint water

4oz (110g) long grain rice

Bundle of parsley

Rind and juice of 6 lemons

Salt and pepper

6 egg yolks

BAKER'S WINE SUGGESTION

A very difficult dish to match. I think that given the huge amount of lemon in this soup the best suggestion would be to serve very chilled Manzanilla Sherry. Outstanding, to my mind, is that made by Javier Hidalgo. It is called La Gitana, (the gypsy) after a lady with whom Javier's great grandfather had a fling! This manzanilla is the lightest in alcohol and is almost like a wine – it is only 2 degrees of alcohol stronger than many a Californian Chardonnay. Marvellously refreshing with any sort of soup and of course as an aperitif. I admit to having drunk four halves of this sherry myself in an evening with no ill effect the following morning.

CORNISH CRAB SOUP WITH CUMIN AND CORIANDER

You need for 8 generous portions:

3lb (1.4k) cooked crab shells
(if you are buying crab just for the
soup, remove the flesh from
cooked claws to use for another
dish but leave the bodies whole
with small legs on)
1 medium onion, finely chopped
5 pints of water
8oz (225g) tomatoes
2 tablespoons tomato purée
1 clove garlic
1oz (25g) each of cumin
and coriander
1 medium potato
4 tablespoons olive oil
Salt and pepper
1 sachet saffron
¼ bottle dry white wine
¼ pt double cream

An aromatic fish soup using your crab shells from another dish, but also certainly worth buying crabs just for this soup. Mussels may also be used as the basis for this soup. This is very much what we feel to be the modern British style, eastern flavours but excellent local materials, the synthesis of international cuisine.

Put crab shells on a tray and roast in hot oven for 30 minutes. Put roughly chopped onion, garlic, potato and tomato in olive oil and cook in the pan you will use for soup until beginning to colour.

Add the shells, water, wine and spices except for saffron.

Simmer gently for 3-4 hours.

Pass through a fine sieve.

Add saffron.

To serve, add a swirl of cream to the tureen and offer croûtons.

PROVENCAL FISH SOUP

Perhaps the most popular soup served at our restaurants over the years. The secret is the quality of the stock, the oil and the garlic. Posh additives can be shellfish, smoked fish or some fish quenelles poached in the soup at the last minute. Sauce rouille, garlic croûtons and aioli (garlic mayonnaise) are good accompaniments.

Dice vegetables finely and soften in olive oil.

Blend the tomatoes in a liquidiser, and add to the vegetables with the fish stock and wine. Simmer for 30 minutes.

Add fish and cook for further 10 minutes. Season to taste.

SAUCE ROUILLE

The business if you like a hot aromatic dash in your soup.

Roughly chop two red peppers with one red chilli. Slice a medium peeled potato, and add to the peppers and blanch for fifteen minutes. Drain, add three cloves of garlic and place in a blender with salt and pepper and a few drops of tabasco. Blend with sufficient olive oil to make a thick paste. Some thicken further with breadcrumbs. Stir into the soup at the table to allow the garlic aroma to waft before the noses of your guests!

You will need for 8 generous portions:

4 tablespoons olive oil

1 onion

1 carrot

1 stick celery

3 cloves garlic

2lb (900g) Italian plum tomatoes

1lb (450g) of monkfish, hake, cod or a mixture

3 pints concentrated fish stock (see Bare Necessities)

½ bottle dry white wine

Level tablespoon of dried 'Herbes de Provence' or similar

Saffron, salt and pepper

BAKER'S WINE SUGGESTION

Another difficult one this: Try an unusual Pinot Grigio from the North of Italy, the best is made by Silvio Jermann. This has a fragrant, almost perfumed nose and enough punch to stand up to the rouille. In the summer I would recommend lashings of the red Estandon from Provence itself, served very cold to disguise the acidity. This is a refreshing quaffing wine. Take no notice of those who say red wine will not 'go' with fish.

LEEK AND CHIVE SOUP

8 generous portions:

2lbs (900g) leeks

2oz (50g) chives

1 medium potato

1 medium onion

2 pints chicken stock

2 pints milk

½ pint cream

Salt, pepper, nutmeg to taste

2oz (50g) butter

These green vegetable soups are a real friend; watercress, leek, spinach, they are so versatile and usually make just as good cold soup as hot. This soup is very close to the classic vichyssoise; the trick with these type of dishes is to cook the green element very lightly to retain the colour, and to use a good chicken stock (see Bare Necessities)

Wash the leeks and chop roughly.

Chop the chives, keeping some back.

Soften the roughly diced onion and potato in the butter without colouring.

Add the stock, milk and seasoning.

Bring to the boil, add the leeks and half the chives and simmer for about five minutes only. Allow to cool, blend thoroughly in a liquidiser or pass through a 'mouli-légumes'.

Check seasoning.

Serve by adding the cream to the tureen and sprinkle finely chopped chives on the top.

BAKER'S WINE SUGGESTION

Despite the onion undertones of leeks and chives this is a delicate flavoured soup. This is the place for a good white Rully such as the Clos St Jacques from Domaine de la Folie or that of Drouhin. The wines really show how good the wines of the Côte Chalonnais can be – it is a pity that a few more producers from this beautiful and overlooked vineyard area are not capable of making wines as good.

SPICED PARSNIP SOUP

The humble parsnip is the root vegetable we really associate with winter food. In this era of air transport that brings us snapper from the Caribbean and beans from Kenya, it is comforting to know that we can look forward to eating some root vegetables only in winter.

The rich sweet flavour of the parsnip really takes to this lightly spiced treatment, to create a warming winter soup.

Soften the onion and potato in the butter.

Add remaining ingredients except the cream.

Chop the parsnips small if you wish to reduce cooking time.

Cook for 45 minutes.

Blend, when cool, in a liquidiser until very smooth - if you like soup with no bits, sieve it in addition.

Add the cream before serving and check the seasoning.

For 8 generous portions:
2lbs (900g) peeled parsnips
1 medium potato chopped
1 onion chopped
5 pints chicken stock
(see Bare Necessities)
2oz (50g) butter
¼ pint double cream
Teaspoon curry powder
Teaspoon ground cumin
Teaspoon ground coriander
Teaspoon ground cardamom

BAKER'S WINE SUGGESTION

Spices and the sweetness of the parsnip make for another powerful Ross combination. Try one of the fruity and spicy wines of Alsace either a Gewurztraminer from Trimbach, whose wines are as clean as his winery, or a Muscat which you should have had as an aperitif - there are few finer pre-dinner drinks.

TOURRIN BORDELAIS

You will need for

8 generous portions:

4 onions

1 carrot

1 stick celery

8oz (225g) peeled chopped
tomatoes

2oz (50g) butter (beef or duck
fat even better)

4 pints good veal stock
(see Bare Necessities)

½ pint young claret

Thyme and bayleaf

4 egg yolks

Salt and pepper

This is the kind of dish one might imagine having been served in a country restaurant in France perhaps twenty years ago, at that auberge in the village square, chanced upon in the early evening, served by one of the family, from a tureen then left on the table. No doubt these places and this type of cooking still exist but we find them rare indeed on our travels.

This is a rich version of a French onion soup, for the winter.

Dice the carrot and celery, and slice the onions.

Heat the butter and fry the vegetables until beginning to colour.

Pour in the stock, tomatoes and seasonings and simmer for one hour. Add the wine and simmer for ten minutes.

To serve, beat the yolks in the bottom of the tureen, take the soup off the boil and ladle into the tureen, whisking vigorously.

If reheating do not allow to boil. Serve with croûtons. The soup is very substantial but the traditional cheese croûtons can still be added to make lunch out of this soup!

BAKER'S WINE SUGGESTION

Marvellously oniony soup is a nightmare to match with wine, especially as the old Bordeaux habit of pouring a glass of wine into the gubbins in the bowl as you lower the level really must be tried. I suggest a full flavoured rosé would be perfect to 'faire chabrot' as this practice is called. Adnams of Southwold stock Ch. Thieuley Clairet a dry, delicious rosé which has the added attraction of the same regional origin as the soup. A lighter rosé such as that produced in Bandol by Domaine Tenpier would also work well.

SALADS

The punk rockers of the new culinary wave of the seventies were the multi-coloured salads in glitzy restaurants. Red lettuce and frisée sprouting in all directions emblazoned with mango slices and kiwi fruit. From this period of soft porn however there has emerged a first course revolution, nurtured by the leading chefs, of elegant salads using delicate young leaves, wild mushrooms, seafood and game enhanced with an array of dressings and oils. One cannot but wonder what all the producers of balsamic vinegar were doing before the entire culinary world wanted their asetic acid and made them overnight lira billionaires.

I have often commented that so many restaurants are so good at first courses and less so at main dishes. Of course herein lies an illusion, in that we naturally like salad type foods; we instinctively feel the quality and texture of green leaves to be wholesome. Our eye is caught by vivid colour, our senses by the

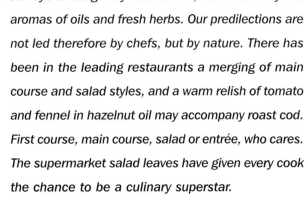

aromas of oils and fresh herbs. Our predilections are not led therefore by chefs, but by nature. There has been in the leading restaurants a merging of main course and salad styles, and a warm relish of tomato and fennel in hazelnut oil may accompany roast cod. First course, main course, salad or entrée, who cares. The supermarket salad leaves have given every cook the chance to be a culinary superstar.

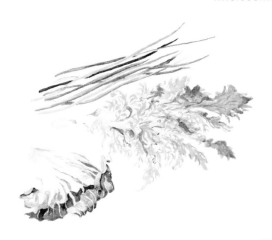

WILD MUSHROOM AND ASPARAGUS SALAD WITH RED ONION AND WATERCRESS

This reads like a special occasion salad, but asparagus in season is not outrageous when sparingly used, and wild mushrooms of the more usual types are now supermarket fare. Mind you if there was the chance of some chanterelles or girolles...! Red onions raw are sweeter than white but leave them out if a less assertive flavour is thought prudent.

Trim the woody stem from the asparagus and blanch for about five minutes if large, and refresh in cold water.

Prepare the salad leaves and watercress discarding the thick stems.

Sauté the mushrooms (carefully washed) in butter and seasoning.

Very thinly slice the onion, combine with the leaves and toss in the dressing. Put this salad on plates first.

Add the asparagus and mushrooms with hazelnuts and chopped flat parsley to decorate.

For 8 first courses:
2lb asparagus (900g)
8oz (225g) selection of wild mushrooms
1 red onion
2 bunches watercress
4oz (110g) chopped toasted hazelnuts
Selection of leaves such as radicchio, cos, rocket, frisée.
Chopped flat leaf parsley
¼ pint vinaigrette (see Bare Necessities) with 2 additional tablespoons hazelnut oil.

BAKER'S WINE SUGGESTION

One of the greatest dishes I ever ate was a combination of Asparagus and Black Truffles at Boyer in Reims. The scent of the two together was quite magnificent. Wild Mushrooms and Asparagus is a similarly magical pairing. A fresh but fragrant number is the answer here so Alsace is probably the best place to focus. Pinot Blanc is an overlooked wine but when young and from a good grower it is delicious. Marcel Deiss is an almost deranged enthusiast: when you visit his cellar he will show you about sixty wines ranging upwards from his impeccably made Pinot Blanc. It is here that I have constantly found the Pinot Blanc with the most fragrance and elegance - well worth searching out.

ROAST AUBERGINE SALAD WITH TOMATO AND FIELD MUSHROOM CROSTINI, YOGHURT AND MINT DRESSING

For eight first course salads:

8 small aubergines

4 tablespoons olive oil

4 plum tomatoes

8 flat field mushrooms

8 slices ciabatta bread or similar

1 clove finely chopped garlic

mixed with 4 tablespoons olive oil

and seasoning for the crostini

Fresh basil or tarragon

Yoghurt and mint dressing

½ pint thick greek yoghurt

Rind and juice of 2 lemons

Handful chopped fresh mint

½ clove garlic, crushed

Seasoning

There is something of a mixture of styles and origins here but that perhaps illustrates the diversity of our sources of inspiration. The very best way of roasting aubergines is in the ashes of the open fire or on the cooler part of the barbeque, where the skin becomes crisp and smokey, the middle remaining soft and piping hot, but if neither is at hand then the oven will do.

This works best using small aubergines that can be served whole and attractively sliced. If using larger ones cut them in half length-ways and roast flat-side down.

Preheat oven to Mk 5 (190C). Brush the skin of the aubergines with the oil and roast for about 30 minutes depending on the size (if using large halves brush the cut side also with the oil.) This stage can be done well in advance, but if keeping overnight in the fridge allow to come back to room temperature before serving.

For the crostini – toast or grill the slices of bread and arrange the sliced tomato and field mushrooms alternately on top and spoon over the garlic, oil and seasoning. Grill under hot grill for 5 minutes.

For the dressing, whisk the ingredients together. To serve, slice the aubergine so that the stalk end is kept whole allowing the aubergine to be spread in an attractive fan shape. Spoon some of the yoghurt dressing over the aubergine serving the remainder separately. Arrange the hot crostini on the plate, still sizzling from the grill, with the fresh herbs over the top.

BAKER'S WINE SUGGESTION

Viognier is a difficult grape to grow and that probably explains why so many winemakers worldwide are attempting to do so. In the south of France many domaines in the Oc are making rather poor examples, although the Domaine Ste Anne is worth seeking out. The real home of the grape is the village of Condrieu in the Northern Rhône but Condrieu is very expensive. The man who really brought Condrieu back to life, George Vemay, is making a Viognier from vineyards on the western fringe of the area and is designating it Vin de Pays des Côtes Rhodaniennes. It is very good. Further south in the Costières de Nîmes a Domaine called Ch Bellecoste makes what is possibly the best non Condrieu Viogniers in France. Again, because the grape is unrecognised by the Appellation Contrôlée regulations this is a Vin de Pays.

MARINATED CHICKEN BREAST SALAD

An excellent summer salad easily adapted to use fish instead. An overhead grill gives an attractive glazed finish to the chicken, and the green salad materials can be changed to suit availability. The fresh coriander and rocket are good because they so splendidly offset the yoghurty acidity of the chicken.

12 hours prior to serving.

Slice the chicken into ¼" thick slices.

Make up a marinade with the remaining ingredients and thoroughly mix in the chicken. Turn twice during the marinating period.

Just prior to serving dress the leaves with a lemony vinaigrette (see Bare Necessities).

Put the chicken pieces still coated in the marinade under a very hot grill for about five minutes, until just browning and just cooked through. Place over the leaves, sprinkle with chopped fresh coriander and lemon zest.

For 8 first courses:
4 medium boneless
chicken breasts
Selection of salad leaves for
eight to include rocket and fresh
coriander

For the marinade:
¼ pint thick yoghurt
Rind and juice of 2 lemons
4 tablespoons olive oil
1 clove garlic, finely chopped
Seasoning
Fresh thyme and flat parsley

BAKER'S WINE SUGGESTION

 An opportunity here to serve a really spicy Gewurztraminer which in addition to going well with dishes like this can be the only wine which remotely suits Chinese and Indian food. Go for a producer of note, Hugel, Trimbach, Deiss, Schlumberger and avoid the insipid wines of the co-operatives.

For 8 first course salads:

*4 medium sized monk fillets
cut into round thin slices well
trimmed (2lb/900g)*

4 back rashers of smoked bacon

1 good head frisée

*2 thick slices white bread cut into
¼" cubes*

2 heads of Belgian chicory

1 clove garlic

For the dressing:

8 tablespoons olive oil

4 tablespoons white wine vinegar

Seasoning

*Sunflower oil or similar to fry the
Croûtons*

*4 tablespoons clarified butter for
the bacon and monkfish*

Fresh chopped parsley

An excellent light lunch or first course which also works well with tuna and other firm meaty fish. The saltiness of the bacon, the bitter chicory, crunchy garlic croûtons.

Prepare the salad materials by slicing the chicory and breaking the frisée into bite size pieces. Make up the dressing. Heat the oil with the peeled garlic clove and fry the cubed bread until crisp – remove onto kitchen paper.

Prior to serving, fry slithers of bacon in butter until crisp and in the same butter fry the monkfish slices for two minutes on each side.

Toss all the ingredients in a salad bowl with the dressing and serve immediately so that the fish is still warm.

BAKER'S WINE SUGGESTION

 A light red from Chinon or Bourgueil would combine with all these ingredients. Make sure that the wine is youngish and served cool. Even the better Loire reds benefit from this, some would say, sacrilegious practise. Names to watch for are Couly Dutheil, and Druet.

SALAD OF ARTICHOKE, CRAB AND FRESH LIMES

In restaurants the lobster has always been the ultimate luxury seafood, having associations I suppose with extravagance, with caviar and champagne. I suspect however that most of us in the food business would happily exchange the lobster for the crab - especially if we were paying! There is a richness and moistness about the crab which makes this a sumptuous summer salad and well worth the effort, especially if one is picking the crabs!

Boil the artichokes in salted water to which has been added 2 halves of lemon and a dash of oil. Cooking time about 20 minutes according to size of chokes (when done a cooking fork should pierce the base effortlessly). For this dish the leaves of the chokes are not needed and may be used for another time, kept in water with lemon juice. Having removed the leaves and 'feathers' in the centre, place each heart in the middle of a plate.

Add the grated rind and juice of the limes to the mayonnaise.

Dress the crabmeat with the mayonnaise and fresh herbs and spoon onto the artichoke hearts.

Arrange the dressed lettuces around the outside and serve immediately.

For 8 first courses:
8 globe artichokes
1lb (450g) of crab meat
(mixed brown and white)
1 lemon
4 fresh limes
8 tablespoons mayonnaise
(see Bare Necessities)
Selection of decorative lettuces
A good vinaigrette
(see Bare Necessities)
2 tablespoons chopped parsley
or chervil

BAKER'S WINE SUGGESTION

 The Semillon grape is not widely grown in France, most of what is, is used to make Sauternes in combination with Sauvignon. In the Antipodes and in America some wineries are making very successful varietal Semillon which has a roundness which would go down well with the Crab and Artichoke and a touch of dry fruitiness in the finish which would partner the lime. Most people who make the wine are entusiasts so you cannot go far wrong. Try Len Evan's Rothbury from the Hunter valley in Australia.

SALADE NICOISE

For 8:

8oz (225g) small new potatoes

1/4 pint vinaigrette

(See Bare Necessities)

24 stoned Niçoise black olives

12 anchovy fillets

8oz (225g) fine french beans,

blanched for 1 minute and

refreshed

6 tomatoes skinned, seeded and

cut into strips.

4 hard-boiled eggs

(6 mins straight into cold water)

Fresh flat parsley

Why include such an old hat salad as this one might ask? Two very good reasons – one it is still a very, very good dish, and two, most restaurants do it wrong. This is the proper way. There is a little care needed in that the potatoes need to be good ones, the beans crisp, the eggs perfectly cooked. Take a little trouble and this is fine cooking. As a main course it becomes a foil for a piece of grilled fish, perhaps salmon or tuna.

Boil the new potatoes until tender. Slice and soak in the vinaigrette while still warm.

Just prior to serving add the beans, tomatoes and olives to the potatoes, toss carefully. Cut the eggs into quarters. Arrange the vegetables on plates and add the eggs and anchovy fillets, and fresh flat parsley.

Grill some french bread in olive oil as an accompaniment.

BAKER'S WINE SUGGESTION

This wonderful summery combination of flavours is difficult to match with wine. In Nice itself the local whites would suit, wines like Cassis and white Bandol but these seem to suffer from not being served on the terrace of the Negresco. A little further to the west the innovative Mas du Daumas Gassac make a white from a mixture of grapes. It is aromatic and full flavoured and would be ideal. Sadly it's not a cheap southern french job but costs over £10 a bottle. If you want something less go to the far South-West of France and buy a wine whose name puts most people off Pacherenc du Vic Bilh; probably the best grower is Alain Brumont whose Ch Bouscasse is an awfully delicious, and again faintly aromatic, wine.

SALAD OF SCALLOPS AND SQUID WITH HAZELNUT DRESSING

As a restaurant cook I have always found it difficult to avoid overusing the 'sure winners' such as fillet steak or turbot, because they are perennially popular, and the cook can do little to spoil such a luxury item. A bit of effort though and less obvious materials can be just as good or even better, at less expense. But the scallop is unique and there is nothing like it for such delicacy and sweet luxury, and that is my excuse if we over indulge. I don't think you can have too much of a good thing when it comes to scallops! The trick is the light cooking of the scallops and squid just before serving.

Prepare your salad materials in fork sized pieces.

Whisk together the dressing ingredients.

The scallops should be cleaned, trimmed of any black bits and sliced in half horizontally. With luck your fishmonger will prepare your squid, if not be brave and proceed as follows:

Under running water pull the head and tentacles away from the body. Remove the grey skin from the body, the clear 'plastic' bone from the centre and slice into thin rounds. The tentacles are quite edible but look slightly off-putting to the squeamish, so assess the guest list! Ten minutes before serving heat the clarified butter, put in the squid, season well, and sauté for two minutes. Cook the scallops similarly but for only one minute.

Toss the salad with the dressing and herbs and arrange the seafood decoratively on top.

For 8 first course salads:

A selection of decorative lettuce –
crispy endive is a good addition
32 scallops with their corals
(sizes vary and so do prices)
2 medium squid or eight of
the baby squid
6 tablespoons olive oil
3 tablespoons hazelnut oil
2 tablespoons wine vinegar
Salt and pepper
Handful chopped chervil
or tarragon
2 tablespoons clarified butter

BAKER'S WINE SUGGESTION

Although we all believe that white Burgundy is made only from the Chardonnay grape there are pockets of both Aligoté and Pinot Gris (known locally as the Pinot Beurot) on the Côte d'Or. These are well worth searching out for they have a distinct and delicious flavour all of their own. Ponsot makes a Morey St Denis Blanc from Aligoté and Thevenot le Brun produces wines in the Hautes Côtes de Nuits from the Pinot Gris. They both have sort of a nutty overtone which would suit the dressing well.

For 8 generous portions:

1lb (450g) calves sweetbreads

4oz (110g) plain flour

Salt and pepper

Coffeespoon ground cumin

Coffeespoon ground coriander

Coffeespoon ground cardamom

Selection of decorative lettuces,

endive and cucumber

6 tablespoons olive oil

3 tablespoons hazelnut oil

4 tablespoons white wine vinegar

4 oz (110g) clarified butter

4 oz (110g) fresh girolles

1 stick chopped celery

1 chopped carrot

A few black peppercorns

I have no doubt that there are plenty of trencherman out there who are not put off the delights of offal by the recent publicity about BSE, and for them and for those times ahead when such scares are forgotten I include this sensational salad. Chicken breast makes a very good alternative but it ain't the same thing!

Other interesting mushrooms will do, but girolles are perfect. This is a good recipe to introduce sweatbreads to the unconverted because by serving them crisp and flavoursome rather than bland and creamy, they are much more appetising.

Place the sweetbreads in a pan of boiling salt water with the celery, carrot and peppercorns and blanch for approximately 15 minutes.

Remove from the pan and carefully trim the 'breads of any membrane. Press under a weight until well cooled. Slice into 1/4" slices.

Prepare a spiced flour by adding the salt, pepper, cumin, cardamom and coriander.

Shortly prior to serving, dress the salad materials with the oil and vinegar and arrange decoratively on large plates.

Roll the spiced sweetbreads in the flour and sauté in hot clarified butter until golden. Season and sauté the girolles in the same way.

Arrange on top of the salad materials.

BAKER'S WINE SUGGESTION

 The earthiness and woody flavours of Girolles calls for something equally earthy. If the pocket allows, try one of the now well made wines of Graves. Since the producers learnt that cool temperature fermentation and short oak ageing were the key to making the Sauvignon and Semillon combination that they use, the wines have improved disproportionately. The best names are of course Haut Brion and Laville Haut Brion but wonderful wines are also made by Ch de Fieuzal and Domaine de Chevalier.

SALAD OF WARM PIGEON BREAST, AVOCADO AND RADICCHIO

There are now very good reared pigeons, or squabs, which are excellent but expensive. The wood pigeon is available for long periods of the year, is inexpensive and extremely delicious; for simplicity ask your butcher for the breasts alone, although the keen and thrifty may like to buy the whole birds to make a game stock with the legs. The avocado has not been to the fore in the nineties but works well here with a lovely colour but avoid slicing until just before needed. The question of how undercooked these birds should be has to be a matter of taste, but the penalty for excessive cooking is a dry and tough meat. Resting the meat after cooking for ten minutes greatly reduces that raw look without drying out the birds.

Have your pigeon breasts ready without the skin. Peel and slice the avocado in long thin slices. Sprinkle with lemon juice. Make your dressing by blending all the ingredients.

Ten minutes before serving grill the pigeon on a high heat for 5 minutes or roast in a hot oven for 5 minutes. Rest the pigeon in a warm place. To serve slice the breasts thinly, they should be just pink in the centre. Interleave the avocado slices with the pigeon and arrange on top of the well dressed radicchio. Pour a little further dressing on top with fresh chopped chives.

Other frilly lettuces may be added, and croûtons add a little crunchy texture.

For 8 first course salads:
The breasts of 8 pigeons
4 ripe avocados
1 large radicchio
1 tablespoon chopped chives

For the dressing:
4 tablespoons walnut oil
8 tablespoons olive oil
4 tablespoons white wine vinegar
2 teaspoons Dijon mustard
Salt and pepper

BAKER'S WINE SUGGESTION

 Here is a good place for a lightish but fruity Italian wine. Perhaps the most consistent of all the better value Italian reds is Dott. Lungarotti's Rubesco Torgiano which you should find in the market-place for about £6. Reliable and easy to drink. As an alternative go for a Chianti Classico from Isole and Olena, Castello di Ama or Monte Vertine who are all on top form at present and who make Chianti which really tastes of the Sangiovese grape.

For 8 first course salads:

1½lbs (675g) fresh goat's cheese

2 beaten eggs

6oz (175g) seasoned flour

6oz (175g) white breadcrumbs

2oz (50g) each chopped tarragon and flat parsley

4oz (110g) clarified butter

Decorative lettuces such as frisée, radicchio, oak leaf.

Vinaigrette (see Bare Necessities)

We have these days stolen a march on the French with our own delicious fresh goat's cheeses. Locally at Bath we have Mary Holbrook's Sleight Farm, and all over the country the cheese specialists are making fine cheeses when unencumbered by EC regulations. This is a simple lunch dish or a starter for a more elaborate meal, and the addition of a grilled croûton of french bread underneath spread with olive oil, is an extra for those of us who are, simply, greedy.

The salty 'logs' are not suitable for this dish.

Keep your cheese very cold until you come to prepare it. Have ready on three separate plates the flour, eggs, and breadcrumbs that have been mixed with the herbs.

Prepare and dress the lettuces on individual plates.

To serve, slice the cheese into ½" thick slices, roll in the flour, egg and breadcrumbs and fry in hot clarified butter. (The grill is also fine for the health conscious.)

Arrange on the salad and serve at once.

BAKER'S WINE SUGGESTION

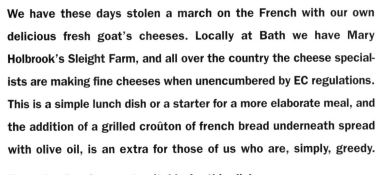

A classic case for a good Beaujolais Cru wine. Try to find something with a little age as contrary to most opinions Beaujolais from a good producer in a good year does age well. Try to avoid factory made Beaujolais from people like Duboeuf who have got too big for their own good and look for wines from single well known domaines like Brouilly Château des Tours, Moulin à Vent au Château des Jacques. There are good negotiants (merchants) wines too, look for Trenel, Drouhin or Dépaneaux.

FISH DISHES

As a restaurant cook, fish beginnings are the essence of the menu. They hold our attention more than any area because there is endless opportunity, so many potential ingredients, so many styles – salads, marinades, soups, pastries, fishcakes, pancakes and pastas, risottos and paellas. Meat main courses are quite restricted by comparison. Most of these fish dishes make simple meals in their own right. Despite our being a seafaring nation we have an increasingly conservative approach to seafood. Gone are the days of oysters, cockles, mussels and whelks being the fare of the common man! These small creatures are excellent appetisers and our fresh taste buds and greed make the prising of these gems from their armour a task to be relished. Who wants to pick a crab for dessert?

Mussels, crabs, mackerel and squid are not desperately extravagant and are worth the little bit of care over freshness. Simplicity is all. The Japanese tell us that there is a new component of taste, alongside sweet, sour and salt called 'umami', responsible for that succulent sweetness in natural foods and, surprise surprise, it is most concentrated in shellfish. Titillate with sensuous seafood first courses and the success of the entire meal is ensured!

CEVICHE OF TURBOT AND LIMES WITH SALAD OF FENNEL AND ORANGES

This is a milder and more luxurious version of the Mexican dish, perhaps better suited to our tastes. It is very similar to Kenneth Bell's caveached salmon that was prepared at Thornbury Castle during the seventies, an English version, and who is to say which came first?

You must have a perfectly fresh turbot, and do not leave it marinating for more than twenty four hours. Use brill or salmon if the budget won't run to turbot which is very, very expensive.

Take the rind off the fruit with a zester and add to the juice and remaining ingredients, mixing thoroughly.

Lay the turbot slices in an open flat dish and cover with the marinade.

Leave for approximately 8-10 hours.

Decorate with chopped chives.

As a side dish with crunch serve a salad of finely sliced fennel with segmented oranges, dressed with vinaigrette flavoured with a little nut oil.

For 8 starters or as a light lunch dish:

1½lb (700g) turbot fillet cut into thin slices
Rind and juice of 4 limes
Rind and juice of 2 oranges
1 finely chopped shallot
1 tablespoon caster sugar
1 glass dry white wine
Salt and pepper
1 chilli, finely chopped
Teaspoon pink peppercorns
Chopped chives

For the salad:

2 oranges
1 fresh fennel bulb
Vinaigrette
Seasoning

BAKER'S WINE SUGGESTION

 It's almost tempting to suggest a glass of Ricard with this amalgam of clean, bright flavours. However if you can't join the flavours try beating them with a buttery Californian Chardonnay from Stags Leap, Frogs Leap, Calera or Ridge.

FRESH SPINACH PASTA WITH SCALLOPS, PRAWNS AND MUSSELS

To make the pasta for

8 first courses:

1lb (450g) plain flour

3 eggs

3oz (75g) spinach purée

(cooked, pressed and blended

from about 8oz (225g) spinach)

2 teaspoons salt

For the seafood:

24 mussels

16 scallops

4oz (110g) prawns (or squid

is also good)

2 tomatoes

1 shallot

¼ pint double cream

¼ pint white wine

Bunch of parsley

A classy pasta dish, where the ingredients could be less extravagant. I like the little clams that they use for this dish in Italy but they seem difficult to get.

Bought pasta is probably the answer unless you have a small pasta machine. Home-made pasta is one of those 'for love' bits of cooking, no need to do it but very satisfying when it works well. Rather in the same way as when serving fine wine, make sure your guests know what they are getting!

Mix the flour, salt and eggs, adding the spinach last.

Knead the dough as for bread.

Rest in the fridge. Set your machine for thin tagliatelle or noodles, having rolled out the dough two or three times to create elasticity.

Clean and cook the mussels with ¼ pint of wine, a chopped shallot and chopped fresh parsley. Boil hard for 30 seconds with a lid on the pan. Remove mussels from shells and retain the cooking liquor.

Add to this liquid two peeled and chopped tomatoes, the scallops and prawns. Poach for 30 seconds and remove the shellfish. When ready to serve, boil the pasta for 5 minutes only. Reduce the sauce, with ¼ pint of cream, add pepper and return the shellfish, Serve over the pasta with chopped parsley.

BAKER'S WINE SUGGESTION

How about some good Italian white wine with the pasta? Yes, there really are quite a few now. What is more they do not break the bank. Almost the best shellfish in Italy comes from the Venetian lagoon, here they would drink a still Prosecco or a Soave. Still Prosecco is impossible to come by outside the Veneto so go for a Soave. The best producers are Pieropan, Pra or even the huge producer Masi.

POT-AU-FEU OF RED MULLET AND CRAYFISH

This dish was cooked by our brigade at The Dorchester when we prepared the lunch with Anton Mosimann for the award of the Egon Ronay Hotel of the Year for Homewood Park in 1987. A glamorous dish for a memorable occasion. Crayfish (the freshwater écrevisse) may be hard to find. Use instead langoustine (Dublin Bay prawn).

There is some license in using the term Pot-au-feu, but the analogy with the real thing is perhaps sufficiently close for us to be excused. Menu writing needs a little 'breadth' from time to time!

Cook the crayfish in boiling water, salted, for 3 minutes. Remove but keep stock. Cool. Keep 8 whole for decorating. Shell the remainder carefully and keep the shells.

Sauté the onion, carrot, celery, garlic and tomato in the olive oil until colouring; add the tomato purée and crushed shells.

Cover with water and wine and simmer for two hours.

Pass the liquid through a fine sieve and reduce to 1½ pints.

Cut the mullet into strips about 2" wide.

Prepare the young vegetables decoratively, blanch and refresh.

Poach the red mullet for a minute only in the crayfish stock with the shallots. Remove the mullet, add cream, seasoning and saffron and reduce to a rich, but not too thick, soup.

At the last minute add the shelled tails, mullet and vegetables with the chopped parsley, and serve in soup bowls, placing a whole crayfish as guardian of each bowl.

Cheaper fish and shellfish of course may be used, perhaps for a practice run?

See your Bank Manager and then assemble for 8 first courses:

32 live crayfish

1 onion finely chopped

1 carrot diced

1 large red mullet (12oz/350g), scaled and filleted

1 stick celery diced

A selection of baby vegetables, such as carrot, mange tout, leek

1 clove garlic finely chopped

1 tomato

2 finely chopped shallots

2 tablespoons olive oil

Small bunch parsley

1 tablespoon tomato purée

¼ pint double cream

¼ bottle dry white wine

Salt, pepper and sachet of saffron

BAKER'S WINE SUGGESTION

The cool climate wines of New Zealand are making a great impression on the market at the moment. A good dry Chardonnay with the super citrus/exotic fruit character which is a feature of good antipodean white wine would go well here. The name of Cloudy Bay has become almost synonymous with New Zealand as far as wine is concerned so look elsewhere. Kumeu River and Wairau River are names to watch out for.

For 8 main dishes:

5lb mussels (2k)

8oz (225g) trimmed squid (see p39 for preparation)

½ bottle white wine

½ pint water

1lb (450g) Arborio rice

2 shallots

2 cloves garlic

2 sachets saffron powder

4 tablespoons olive oil

4 tablespoons double cream (more olive oil if you don't want cream)

Salt and pepper – remember the mussels are quite salty

Bunch of parsley

If you think that risotto is about a quick way of using up the Sunday joint, forget it. Think things Italian; style, clothes, red Alfa Spyders and home–made pasta. Can you imagine an Italian driving an Allegro or making risotto from cold lamb?

First the rice – it has to be a proper risotto rice such as Arborio.

The mussels – you could take a short cut and add cooked mussels but the flavour of this dish comes from the mussel cooking juice being used in the risotto.

Finely chop the shallot and garlic, sweat in half the olive oil until soft in a large pot. Add half the wine and water, bring to the boil and add the mussels, steam with lid on for about two to three minutes shaking the pan until the mussels are all open. Pour off the liquor through a fine sieve or muslin, and reserve.

To the remaining olive oil add the rice, stir thoroughly. Add the remaining liquids slowly as the rice cooks, adding more as the rice soaks up the wine and water. In all about twenty minutes until the rice is soft but not overcooked. Slice the squid into very thin strips and add to the reserved mussel liquor with the saffron and cream. Cook for two minutes and add to the risotto with the shelled cooked mussels. A few mussels left in the shell look decorative around the dish. Add fresh parsley, serve immediately.

BAKER'S WINE SUGGESTION

Fish risotto needs fairly powerfully flavoured white wine with a bit of bite. In southern California several winemakers have been trying out Rhône varietals to great effect. The principal proponent is Randall Grahm who makes a delicious Malvasia, ideal as an aperitif but more interestingly a blended white called Il Pescatore. This is ideal with all fish and has the weight to go with this particular starter. He also makes a more expensive white from Marsanne called Le Sophiste, this comes with a plastic top hat instead of a capsule – all Grahms wines have faintly amusing, rather silly labels.

HOT SCALLOP TART WITH CHICORY AND ORANGES

Originally an idea of Roger Vergé of the Moulins des Mougins to which I have added the concept of the puff pastry case to give it a more northern feel! The secret is the acidity of the oranges balancing the sweetness of the scallops, the chicory being crisp and a little bitter. This recipe works best as individual tarts.

Preheat your oven to gas MK 7 (220C).

Trim and wash scallops and slice in half horizontally.

Roll out puff pastry to ¼" thick (this will rise like a vol-au-vent case) and cut out 8 round tart bases about 6" across

Score with the point of a small knife about ¼" in from the edge around the case to create a lid when the case is cooked. Chill.

Place on a baking sheet, brush with milk and cook for 15 minutes until risen and golden. Carefully remove the lid and set aside. Discard any underdone pastry from inside.

Poach the scallops for 30 seconds in the stock, then remove.

Add the wine, rind and juice of the oranges and reduce by fast boiling to a rich velvet consistency. Add the cream and check seasoning of the sauce. Add the chicory and scallops at the last minute. Fill the tart cases and replace the pastry lids.

Serve any additional sauce around the tarts.

For 8 tarts:

About 24 medium size fresh scallops

1lb (450g) puff pastry (see Bare Necessities)

¼ pint dry white wine

¼ pint concentrated fish stock (see Bare Necessities)

Grated rind and juice of 2 oranges

¼ pint double cream

1 large head of belgian chicory finely sliced

Salt and pepper

BAKER'S WINE SUGGESTION

Super combination of tastes and textures which needs a dry, flowery wine like Sancerre or Pouilly Fumé. These have become somewhat of restaurant clichés in recent years and because the demand is so high there is a lot of junk on the market. Look out for Sancerres from Vatan, Vacheron and Bourgeois and Pouilly Fumé from anyone called Daguneau (there are three or four lots).

For 8 first courses:

8 thick slices of ciabatta bread or similar

¼ pint olive oil

1 onion finely chopped

2 cloves garlic finely chopped

2 tomatoes peeled and chopped

1 small red pepper finely chopped

1 medium squid trimmed and chopped into small pieces (see pg 39 for squid preparation)

2lb(1K) steamed mussels (keep the cooking liquor for the sauce)

1lb (450g) prawns, the best that you can afford!

1lb (450g) monktail fillet cut into small chunks

1 glass white wine

Seasoning

Fresh basil and thyme

Bruschetta and crostini have been two of the buzz words in restaurants of the nineties. It is fair to say that bruschetta sounds a bit more sexy than olive oil toast, but that is more or less what it is! The bread acquires that lovely charred taste if cooked on a griddle or char-grill, but otherwise use an overhead grill. Putting olive oil soaked bread in the toaster could be an inflammatory method!

Other seafoods do just as well, but stick to the firm textures so you do not finish up with overcooked white fish – the idea is to have lots of little firm bits of seafood with plenty of colour.

Soften the onion and garlic in half of the oil, add the pepper, cook for a further few minutes. Add the wine and an equal amount of mussel liquor or water, add the fish and cook for just a few minutes (it may be best to add the smallest items such as the prawns at the last minute.)

Remove the fish, reduce the sauce to a rich consistency, add the tomatoes and herbs, put back the fish.

Brush the remaining oil over the bread and grill until crispy and charred. Spoon over the fish, and serve immediately before the bruschetta goes soggy.

BAKER'S WINE SUGGESTION

This needs an oaky Chardonnay from California, try to get some Mondavi Reserve or alternatively some Swanson. Both have well used oak and not too buttery an aftertaste. Both are quite able to stand the powerful flavours of this aromatic dish.

SEARED SALMON FILLET WITH PRAWN AND ANCHOVY MAYONNAISE, CHICORY SALAD

That chicken of the sea, the versatile farmed salmon may not be the purist's choice, but for pro cooks it is a great medium for sauces, oily enough to take grilling well, inexpensive, and carefully cooked still as flavoursome as many more extravagant fish. This dish is essentially raw, so make sure your fish is really fresh.

Combine the ingredients for the mayonnaise and keep in the fridge.

Make a salad of sliced chicory, fresh tarragon, dressed with the hazelnut oil and orange juice. Arrange on plates already for the fish, which must be served pronto!

Lay the slices on a flat tray and sprinkle with lemon juice, season well.

Heat the oil until beginning to smoke, and put in a few slices at a time to keep the oil hot. Sear on each side for twenty seconds only and serve immediately with the mayonnaise.

You may like to make a smart criss-cross pattern on the fish if you have a cast-iron griddle, just beware the fish does not stick, by oiling the griddle first.

For 8:

2lb (900g) salmon fillet, cut into sixteen ¼" thick slices
4 tablespoons olive oil
Juice of two lemons

For the mayonnaise:

½ pint mayonnaise
(see Bare Necessities)
4oz (110g) peeled prawns (dry)
8 chopped anchovy fillets
2 tablespoons chopped dill

For the salad:

4 heads belgian endive
Bunch fresh tarragon
2 tablespoons hazelnut oil
2 tablespoons fresh orange juice

BAKER'S WINE SUGGESTION

Salmon demands something rich like chardonnay but with the prawn and anchovy accompaniment try one of the wonderful un-oaked Chablis wines of Dauvissat or Louis Michel. Chablis should not taste of oak but should be clean, fresh and lively with good acidity and a penetrating, lengthy finish. Oak fermented and aged wines should stay in the Côte d'Or where they belong!

ARBROATH SMOKIE FISHCAKES WITH LEMON AND DILL CREAM

For 8 first courses:

1lb (450g) smokie fillet lightly poached in milk

8oz (225g) mashed potato

2 eggs

2oz (50g) butter

1 tablespoon each chopped dill and parsley

Pinch of nutmeg

Salt and pepper

Breadcrumbs

For the lemon and dill cream:

¼ pint mayonnaise

(see Bare Necessities)

2½ fl oz whipped cream

Tablespoon chopped dill

Rind and juice of 2 lemons

Those dedicated smokers of baby haddock in the North- East would perhaps be perturbed to know that their wonderful Arbroath smokies were being used for fishcakes. We, of course, now view fishcakes as not just a way of using up the leftovers but as a culinary treat in their own right. Their abuse by restaurants should not discourage you from this ultimate fishcake. (Try with poached eggs for breakfast)

Poach your smokie very lightly to retain the moisture – five minutes for 1lb.

Make a smooth mashed potato and beat in the butter and eggs. Flake the haddock and mix into the potato with the herbs and seasonings. Allow to cool.

Roll the fishcakes on a floured board, coat with breadcrumbs and fry in hot clarified butter until golden.

For the lemon and dill cream:

To ¼ pint of mayonnaise fold in lightly whipped cream and chopped dill. Add zest and juice of lemons. Chill.

CARPACCIO OF TUNA WITH RELISH OF LEEKS AND TOMATO IN BALSAMIC VINEGAR

I have had several people comment that they never realised that tuna could be fresh and I think that many thought of tuna for years as chunky, dry lumps out of a tin. The real thing is succulent and delicate, but needs to be undercooked or in this case just marinated.

This dish is the creation of Matthew Prowse, chef at the Olive Tree, and was an entry for a competition where it was highly acclaimed!

With a very sharp knife slice the tuna paper thin, easier if it has been chilled in the freezer but not frozen. In a large flat dish lay out the slices. Blanch the leeks for 30 seconds, refresh in cold water, add to the chopped tomatoes and lime segments, shallot and garlic. Whisk up the oil and vinegar, seasoning, sugar and herbs, mix with the tomatoes and leek, and pour over the tuna slices. Marinate for about 3 hours. The fish should look 'rare'. If you like a cooked effect marinate for longer.

Serve with a crisp salad of endive and radicchio dressed with hazelnut oil.

For 8 first courses:

2lb (900g) fresh tuna loin

6 seeded, skinned and chopped tomatoes

1 medium leek finely diced

4 fresh limes, segmented

1 shallot, finely chopped

6 tablespoons olive oil

6 tablespoons balsamic vinegar (extravagant, could be sherry vinegar instead)

1 clove chopped garlic

Salt and pepper

1 tablespoon caster sugar

Fresh tarragon and basil

BAKER'S WINE SUGGESTION

Tuna is a meaty fish and can take red or white wine. Why not serve Red and White Sancerre from the same producer? There are several good Sancerre makers, Henri Bourgeois and Jean Vatan make good wines but for the real McCoy it is Vacheron every time. His Red wine is from the Pinot Noir grape and is aged in two and three year old oak casks from famous Burgundian houses like the Domaine de la Romanee Conti.

WATERCRESS PANCAKES FILLED WITH SAFFRON CRAB

For 8 portions of small pancakes:

Purée of watercress

1 small onion chopped

2oz (50g) unsalted butter

¼ pint double cream

¼ pint milk

10 bunches watercress
without stalks

For the pancakes:

8 eggs

4oz (110g) unsalted butter melted

6 tablespoons plain flour

Oil for cooking pancakes

For the filling:

1 large crab cooked
(or 12oz/350g crabmeat)

A sachet powdered saffron

4 tablespoons double cream

Parsley, salt and pepper

Pancakes are one of those culinary building blocks whose versatility makes them useful in every area of the menu. Savouries or puddings, vegetarian and fish, and here green pancakes look most attractive and a luxury crab filling is used. For a fishy first course we have also used smoked haddock – excellent. The green effect is possible with spinach but beware the large amount of water in the spinach and drain well.

Soften the onion in the butter.

Add the cream and milk and bring to the boil.

Add watercress and cook for 2 minutes. Blend in a liquidiser and sieve. Make the batter by blending ingredients in a liquidiser until smooth. Combine this mixture with watercress purée. After resting the batter for 1 hour make 16 wafer thin pancakes and set aside.

Mix together brown and white meat of crab. Place in a pan and season with salt and pepper, saffron, cream and parsley. Heat gently until bubbling. Spoon this mixture into pancakes, fold decoratively and serve with any extra filling lightened with a little extra cream to make a sauce.

If there is spare watercress purée this makes an attractive alternative sauce

AVOURY BEGINNINGS

Memories of early visits to France as a teenager are of charcuterie, wonderful pâtés and terrines, sausages, rillettes and hams. We simply have no tradition of this regional co-operation between producer, butcher and chef central to the French and Italian local food economy. Our own brawn and black pudding have never spread much beyond their Northern origins, curious as we all go to France and relish their delicacies. There is a certain detachment about the British and their food. We don't seem to be really keen to get very involved in how foods are produced and what they contain, best to eat these things abroad where you don't ask. Such an attitude has certainly reaped a cruel harvest in the nineties for our meat industry.

On a lighter note of course we are the arch plagiarists in that we delight in the borrowing of all that is charming about others cooking. Our savoury tastes are satisfied by pasta, pastries and pâtés from all over the place. As with wine, we are the world's entrepôt for culinary fashion and quality. Armed with the food processor we now enjoy mousselines, pastries and soufflés that have previously been the preserve of professionals, and we have discovered that many of these things are pretty simple. Perhaps soufflés are just a load of hot air!

AUBERGINE, MOZZARELLA AND PARMA HAM FRITTERS

This is a recipe inspired by Franco Taruschio of The Walnut Tree at Abergavenny. My excuse for occasionally borrowing a dish from another chef is that I have no doubt that my dishes have been borrowed by plenty of others!

Soften the diced vegetables in olive oil, add the tomatoes and wine and cook for 30 minutes; pass through a mouli, or sieve.

Slice the aubergine about ¼" thick, sprinkle with olive oil and grill or fry until golden. Place a slice of cheese and ham between aubergine slices, roll these 'sandwiches' in the flour, egg and breadcrumb mixture and fry in clarified butter until crisp. Lay on kitchen paper, serve with the tomato sauce above.

For eight first courses:

4 medium aubergines

1lb (450g) mozzarella

4oz (110g) Parma ham sliced

4oz (110g) seasoned flour

2 eggs

4oz (110g) breadcrumbs

for the coating.

For a tomato sauce:

1 onion

1 stick celery

1 carrot

8oz (225g) tinned tomatoes

¼ pint dry white wine

Basil, thyme and seasoning

CHEESE BEIGNETS WITH TOMATO AND SWEET PEPPER SAUCE

For 8:

½ pint water

8oz (225g) butter, cut into pieces

6oz (175g) flour

1 teaspoon salt

3 eggs

8oz (225g) grated cheddar

For the sauce:

1 onion

1 clove garlic

2 red peppers

4 tomatoes

2 tablespoons tomato purée

¼ pint chicken stock or water

1 glass white wine

Tablespoon caster sugar

Seasoning, basil and thyme

½ red chilli

BAKER'S WINE SUGGESTION

There is a little known area of North West Spain with the somewhat Spanish name of Toro. They make light but amazingly fruity wines and call them Vino Joven. A particularly good producer is called Bodegas Frutas Villar whose Tinto Muruve is a wonderful wine, bursting with exuberant young fruit and with enough depth to stand up to the red peppers in the sauce.

This recipe is really here as a reminder of the great versatility of choux pastry. This classic beignets soufflés au fromage is but one version of all those choux variations, the gougère from Burgundy, sweet choux buns and éclairs, St Honoré. This recipe works well also with crab substituted for the cheese. Take care with the deep frying, and make sure that the beignets are cooked by waiting until they roll over in the oil.

To make the choux paste, bring the salted water to the boil, drop in the butter and simmer until the butter is dissolved and foaming. Pour in the flour in a stream and beat vigorously with a wooden spoon until the paste is smooth and coming away from the sides of the pan. Put back over the heat, stirring, for a few minutes to dry out the paste. Add the eggs one by one beating each in to make a smooth paste. Add the grated cheese. The mixture can be kept at this stage overnight or used immediately.

To cook, bring sufficient oil with enough depth to deep fry the beignets to a frying temperature. If using a conventional pan take great care that the pan is large enough to allow some foaming of the oil without overflowing the pan. Drop in large teaspoonfuls of the mixture, a few at a time, frying for about 3-4 minutes, waiting for them to turn over. Remove onto kitchen paper.

For the Tomato and Sweet Pepper Sauce: soften the chopped onion and clove of garlic in olive oil; add chopped red peppers, chopped tomatoes, tomato purée, chicken stock or water, glass white wine, sugar, seasoning and fresh basil and thyme. A half red chilli is a good addition for a spicier sauce. Simmer for half an hour and pass through a mouli-légumes, or liquidise for a thicker paler sauce. Serve the beignets very hot on the sauce.

CHICKEN LIVER TART WITH MUSTARD AND TARRAGON

The humble chicken liver, so rarely recognised in the pages of the books by the star chefs is of course excellent when coming from free-range poultry and not frozen before use.

Many cooks suggest soaking chicken livers in milk or water but I find this makes them sloppy to cook. Better to wash them, trim any green bits or white sinew and pat them dry with kitchen paper.

Roll out the pastry to ⅛" thick and cut 8 suitable rounds. Butter the cases carefully and line with the pastry.

Remember to cut the pastry oversize to avoid stretching when fitting into the case.

In a medium (Mk4 180C)oven bake the cases blind using baking beans or rice in foil. When cooked (about 10 minutes) remove beans and dry out for further 2-3 minutes. Allow to cool before turning out the cases onto plates.

For the filling, cut the livers in half, heat the clarified butter and sauté the livers with shallot for 2-3 minutes until firm to the touch and just pink inside. Remove and keep warm.

Add to the pan the stock, cream, wine and mustard and reduce to rich texture. Season and add the tarragon.

Place the livers in the cases and spoon over the sauce.

This recipe calls for individual tart cases with removable bases.
For 8 individual tarts:
1lb (450g) short pastry
(see 'Bare Necessities')
1lb (450g) fresh chicken livers
½ pint chicken stock
(see Bare Necessities)
¼ pint double cream
¼ pint dry white wine
2 tablespoons wholegrain mustard
1 shallot finely chopped
Tablespoon chopped tarragon
2oz (50g) clarified butter
Salt and pepper

BAKER'S WINE SUGGESTION

 Another blockbuster combination of flavours and another which would suit an Alsace wine very well. When they eat Fole Gras there they drink Tokay of a middle range sweetness so, go for a great Hugel Reserve Personnelle. Hugel are class at making this sort of perfumed wine. Ignore those who say that they make only commercial stuff.

DUCK AND PLUM TERRINE WITH CUMBERLAND SAUCE

You will need, for a terrine 4"
deep and 12" long (typical le
creuset size):

12oz (350g) trimmed duck meat
(best to buy legs)

8oz (225g) smoked streaky bacon

8oz (225g) belly pork

4oz (110g) plums

1 medium onion

2 cloves garlic

2oz (50g) butter

Rind and juice 2 oranges

2 eggs

Teaspoon thyme and oregano

4oz (110g) back bacon rashers
for lining the terrine

1 glass white wine

10 juniperberries crushed

For the Cumberland sauce:

1 shallot, finely chopped

Rind and juice of 4 oranges and
2 lemons

8oz (225g) red-currant jelly

1 glass port

2 tablespoon wine vinegar

This is a straightforward recipe for a coarse terrine easily adapted to other meats. The principle of cooking terrines is that the meat cooks very slowly in the fat. A lean terrine is really not practicable, but the surplus melted fat may be discarded if so wished. One advantage of chefs using so many duck breasts is that there is always an inexpensive supply of legs!

If you have time, marinate the meats in the wine, herbs and orange juice for twenty-four hours prior to cooking. Put the duck, pork and streaky bacon through a fine mincer. Soften the onion and garlic in the butter, add to the meat. Simmer the stoned plums in the white wine until soft and set aside.

Add the remaining ingredients to the meat except the back rashers, mix thoroughly and season well. If you wish to test the flavour fry a little of the mixture in a pan to taste.

To line the terrine tap out the back rashers until paper thin laying the strips in the terrine to provide an overlap to cover the top.

Add half the mixture, then the plums in the wine, then the remaining mixture. Fold over the bacon lining, then place the terrine in a tray of hot water and cook in a low oven Gas MK1 (140C) for 1½ hours. Test by pushing a skewer or thin knife into the centre, from which the juice should be clear. Cool with a weight on the terrine.

For the Cumberland sauce: put all the ingredients into a heavy bottomed pan and reduce by simmering until the sauce is beginning to thicken, then chill.

WARM GOAT'S CHEESE AND HAZELNUT TART

Perhaps instead of slaving over a hot stove for twenty years we should have been breeding goats, as the popularity of goat's cheese seems boundless. This recipe is for a little delicate quiche where the goat's cheese is a bit more subtle than the usual cheddar and tomato treatment.

For a deep flan dish, roll out the pastry, chill and bake 'blind' using baking beans or rice at Mk4 (180C) for 15 mins. Allow to cool. In a processor blend the other ingredients until smooth. Pour into the flan case and bake at Mk4 (180C) for about 30 mins. Check that the top of the tart is not browning too quickly, if so cover with foil or turn down the oven. When set sprinkle over the chopped nuts. Serve with watercress salad.

For eight generous slices you will need:

8oz (225g) rich shortcrust pastry (see Bare Necessities)

6 whole eggs

3 yolks

½ pint double cream

¼ pint milk

8oz (225g) fresh goat's cheese

Salt, pepper and grated nutmeg

2oz (50g) toasted chopped hazelnuts

BAKER'S WINE SUGGESTION

Although one could drink a white wine like a Riesling or Muscat from Alsace with this dish I think it really needs red wine, not too powerful but with nice sweet fruit. Most New Zealand red wines are a bit weak and weedy but a Cabernet or better still a Cabernet Merlot from Matua Valley would fit the bill here. A lightish Pinot say from the Hautes Côtes de Nuits or the Hautes Côtes de Beaune would also be a good combination. Watch out for the wines of the Gros family or for those of Jayer-Gilles.

POTATO GNOCCHI WITH SAFFRON COURGETTES

For 8:

2lb (900g) potatoes, boiled drained and passed through a mouli or mashed

8-12oz (225-350g) plain flour

2 eggs

Seasoning

2oz (50g) fresh parmesan

2 medium courgettes

¼pt chicken stock

sachet saffron

4 tablespoons double cream

All the shop-bought and pre-prepared pastas tend to remove the incentive to making pasta. Who is going to tell the difference and recognise the effort. Gnocchi are the exception since they must be cooked as soon as they are made, your guests know you have gone to the trouble! Despite the fashion for polenta I still prefer the potato gnocchi; they are a little tricky because the type of potato affects the quantity of flour needed, so start the mix with the minimum and poach one to test the texture.

Beat the flour and eggs into the potato quickly and lightly, don't overwork. Roll out into a sausage on a floured board, cut into 2" cylinders. Poach a tester in simmering salted water for 2-3 minutes. If too fragile add a little more flour.

Grate two courgettes on the largest side of the grater. In an open sauté pan poach the courgettes in enough chicken stock (or water with a little white wine) to just cover them. Add a sachet of saffron, seasoning and a little cream. Only cook for a few minutes.

To serve, poach the gnocchi, drain well and place on top of the saffron courgettes, scatter with flaked fresh parmesan.

BAKER'S WINE SUGGESTION

Gnocchi demands Italian wine but something not too strong. Many Italian winemakers have imported the Sauvignon grape and have used it, often in combination with a little new oak. Both Gaja in Piedmont (whose wine is called Alteni di Brassica), and Avignonesi in Tuscany (whose wine is called Il Vignola) make excellent examples. The cheaper of the two at just about a tenner is the Avignonesi example.

ROAST MEDITERRANEAN VEGETABLES WITH OLIVE CROSTINI

Some dishes come and go with fashion and are quickly forgotten, especially if they were difficult to do. These roast vegetable dishes however are so simple and wholesome that they will be absorbed into British cuisine as comfortably as their national bedfellow, fresh pasta.

Use any combination of vegetables but that sunny flavour comes from the aubergine, peppers and garlic. Roasting as a description has been hijacked by chefs, grilling with olive oil gives a very similar result. Make the day before if possible.

Sprinkle aubergine with oil and roast in hot oven till brown then add roughly chopped courgettes and onion and continue roasting until courgettes are just tender. Meanwhile put the quartered peppers under a hot grill until the skin is well charred and peels easily. Add to the other vegetables. Peel and pip the tomatoes, add when cool along with the garlic, fresh herbs, olives and oil.

Blend the olives with oil and a few anchovy fillets and pepper to make a 'tapenade' to spread on the crostini. Spread french bread croûtons with olive oil and grill until crisp, add the tapenade and serve with the vegetables at room temperature

For 8:

1 large aubergine, chunkily diced

2 courgettes

1 red pepper, skinned and quartered

1 green pepper, ditto

1 red onion sliced

1 tablespoon each chopped fresh basil and thyme

2 cloves chopped garlic

4 skinned and pipped tomatoes

¼ pint of best olive oil budget permits

Pepper

4oz (110g) stoned black olives

(2oz being for the paste for the crostini)

1oz (25g) anchovy fillets

BAKER'S WINE SUGGESTION

The Pays d'Oc has changed massively over the last ten years, particularly during the recession. French wine makers have worked out that they must compete with the New World wines which have taken so much of their market. Many domaines have been making successful wines, none more so than the Domaine Virginie near Beziers. Everyone is making Chardonnay and Sauvignon and those of Virginie are very good but their most exciting white wine is from the Rousanne, a variety grown in the Rhône. This has sufficient punch to deal with the roast of the vegetables and the strength of the olive crostini.

ROQUEFORT AND WALNUT SOUFFLE

You will need for 8 individual
soufflés, in small ramekins:
3oz (75g) butter
4oz (110g) plain flour
1 pint milk
8 eggs
6oz (175g) grated roquefort
Seasoning, including nutmeg
4oz (110g) chopped walnuts

I am not sure that the soufflé should be regarded as a very special dish. It is after all largely flour, egg, and hot air. It is also very dull when done badly and therefore for the restaurant we tend to stick to those with robust flavours, which still impress even if there has been a slight lapse with the timing!

This is a variation on the cheese soufflé theme in which stilton may be used as an alternative. At home the cook has the great advantage over the restaurant – they can ensure that the guests are at the table and even keep them waiting if necessary. Although less spectacular the individual soufflés cook more quickly and are less prone to collapse.

Melt the butter, add the flour and cook the roux for five minutes without letting it colour. Gradually add the warmed milk, using a whisk to prevent any lumps. Simmer the sauce until smooth and thick, allow to cool a little.

Meanwhile carefully separate the whites and yolks. Beat the yolks and add to the sauce. Add the cheese and seasoning and stir over a low heat to dissolve the cheese. Allow to cool. Mix in the walnuts. Whisk the whites in a very clean bowl until holding their shape, but before they become granular. Stir in a little of the whites into the mixture vigorously, and then very carefully fold in the remainder.

Butter the dishes well and fill threequarters full.

Sprinkle a few chopped walnuts on the top and bake at gas MK 6 (200C) until well risen and holding their shape – about 25 minutes.

BAKER'S WINE SUGGESTION

Controversial writers would suggest a light Sauternes or a Muscat from Frontignan or Beaumes de Venise with this. That would be fine if you were going to eat and drink nothing more after the soufflé. However sweet wine does coat the palate so its better to try to find a wine which will have a richness and flavour for this dish. Although it is expensive Condrieu of Ch. Grillet from the Viognier grape made in the Rhône valley would have the right sort of punch and the richness too.

HOT TART OF QUAILS' EGGS WITH LEEKS AND SAFFRON

A sumptuous bird's nest. Just occasionally a rich dish is rather welcome, perhaps to be followed by some simple roast meat or grilled fish. Small pullets' eggs will do if you cannot get the quails' eggs, but it is the smallness of the eggs that makes the dish entertaining.

Roll out the pastry to a sheet of about ¼" thickness – when risen the tart should be at least 1" high.

Cut out 8 rounds with a saucer. Glaze the top of the pastry avoiding the edge, and bake in a hot oven (Mk 7 220C) until risen and golden.

Whilst the tart cases are baking, in an open pan reduce the wine and stock. When reduced by half add the cream, saffron and seasoning to make a rich sauce.

Prepare the leek in fine strips or 'juliennes', blanched in salted water for 20 seconds and refreshed in cold water.

The quails' eggs should be poached in salted acidic water for one minute and removed to drain on a paper towel.

To serve, remove the centre of the top of the tart cases. Lay the quails' eggs in the base of the nests, spoon over the hot sauce. Place the leeks on the top, and put each tart under a hot grill for a few seconds to crispen the leeks.

For 8 individual tarts:
1lb (450g) puff pastry
(see Bare Necessities)
24 quails eggs
1 medium leek
½ pint chicken stock
(see Bare Necessities)
¼ pint double cream
1 sachet saffron
¼ pint dry white wine
Seasoning
1 egg for glazing pastry

BAKER'S WINE SUGGESTION

Vouvray is a much derided drink, mainly because the producers are never quite sure how to label the wines. You can get ultra dry wines that are described as Demi Sec and flabby sweetish wines called the same. The answer, as is normally the case, is to go for the names of the producers. Perhaps the finest producer is Huet. His Clos de Bourg is an expression of how Chenin Blanc should be made.

VENISON AND JUNIPER RISSOLES WITH SWEET AND SOUR LEEKS

For 8 first courses:

*2lb(900g) minced roe shoulder
(ask your butcher to do this, they
often sell venison pie mix which is
just as good, but make sure there
is no sinew left in, as this dish
will not be cooked for very long)
4oz (110g) streaky bacon
1 medium finely chopped onion
2 cloves finely chopped garlic
1 tablespoons ground juniperberry
4 tablespoons plain flour
3 eggs
Seasoning
1 tablespoon soft brown sugar
1 tablespoon fresh thyme*

For the sweet and sour leeks:

*1 medium leek
½ pint chicken stock
6 tablespoons white wine vinegar
1 tablespoon soft brown sugar
1oz (25g) butter*

This is about as superior a burger as you will get, and in this era of frenzied concern over meat, the roe deer looks as politically correct a choice as one could make. We have served this as a winter beginning but it makes a robust main dish if the rissoles are made a little larger, but remember to increase the cooking time.

Fry the bacon, garlic and onion until soft and browned, with the seasonings and juniper. Mix in well with the meat. Add the flour and the eggs to form stiff paste. Chill. On a floured board roll into rissoles or small cakes and chill until ready to cook.

For the sweet and sour leeks: finely slice a medium leek into 'juliennes' (matchsticks) and blanch in boiling water for one minute, refresh. Reduce stock with wine vinegar and soft brown sugar, by half. Whisk in a knob of butter, and just prior to serving add the leeks.

To serve, fry the rissoles in hot oil for five minutes each side until brown and crisp. Leave in a warm oven for ten minutes before serving to ensure that the cakes are evenly cooked. Serve on top of the sweet and sour leeks.

BAKER'S WINE SUGGESTION

 Venison and juniper are both strong flavours – they go exceedingly well with each other and demand a strongish wine. Good, simple Côtes du Rhône is difficult to come by when ready to drink so its always advisable to buy a few cases of Jaboulet's Parallel 45 or Guigals seriously underpriced Côtes du Rhône and put them away under the stairs for dishes like this. In a good vintage they need five years at least to be ready to drink.

FISH DISHES

The Brits seem somewhat schizophrenic about fish. We lost the cod war without a whimper, and fresh fish shops in cities such as our own have turned bank managers as cold as their slabs. Yet in restaurants we can't get enough of it, and seem happy to pay twenty pounds for a Dover sole. Perhaps the supermarkets will have changed things for the better and encouraged, with their fresh fish counters, a return to fish retailing by selling fish in amongst the cornflakes and carrots, so no courage is required to cross the fishmonger's threshold!

These recipes are intended to be very simple, encouraging for the faint-hearted. A few musts: get the fish shop to do the preparation, cook fish for as short a time as you dare, and keep fish dishes for occasions when the cook's attention can be 100%!

Given that every chef in the land has been serving fish by the trawler load recently it is not surprising that some species are rare and expensive, however most recipes are easily adapted to a less fashionable fish. Try grey mullet instead of bass, hake instead of turbot, gurnard instead of monkfish. Poaching fish is difficult and disperses flavour into the poaching water, so try cooking fish gently in olive oil, baking in the oven and grilling. Curiously the strong flavour of chargrilling seems to enhance the taste of fish, especially the oily ones, and the meaty fish such as tuna and swordfish are delectable on the barbecue. With all the up to the minute oils, vinegars and herbs now available to us, forget all the elaborate sauces and think freshness!

STEAMED SEA BASS WITH FENNEL, TOMATO AND FRESH SORREL HOLLANDAISE

Bass is frighteningly expensive, although the small farmed fish are good value. It is still worth the extra investment for that special occasion, and a whole large fish is a fabulous sight. Make sure that your fishmonger cleans and scales the fish well, or if doing it yourself be careful of the spines as these give an unpleasant wound if one is stabbed. The sorrel gives a sharp tang to the hollandaise, making it less rich.

The bass should be filled with the parsley stalk and lemons, well seasoned, with the butter poured over the fish. If you do not have a suitable steamer place a cake rack over a tray filled with water. Bring to the boil. Steam for seven minutes to the pound, in the oven on a low heat, covering the fish with foil. Prepare the fennel and tomato by slicing one bulb of fennel into fine strips, blanching in salt water and refreshed in cold. Skin, de-seed and slice the tomatoes finely.

To complete the dish carefully season the fennel and tomato with lemon juice, heat carefully, and arrange alongside the bass, or on each plate if one is going to portion the fish in the kitchen. Serve the hollandaise separately

For 8 main courses:

a 6lb (2.8K) sea bass

4oz (110g) melted butter

Bunch fresh parsley

2 fresh lemons

1 bulb of fennel

6 plum tomatoes

For the sauce:

(see Bare Necessities for hollandaise sauce) then, to one pint of hollandaise add small bunch of shredded sorrel leaves, raw, at the last minute

BAKER'S WINE SUGGESTION

Sea Bass has become a very fashionable fish in exactly the way that white Burgundy has become a very fashionable wine. The fish is perfect for Meursault the richer and finer the better. Watch out for the wines of Lafon, Ampeau, Javillier and Coche Dury. Lesser growers wines give a less rich impression and should be avoided.

COULIBIAC OF SALMON

For 8 main courses:

2lb (900g) of lightly cooked salmon flesh

3 hard-boiled eggs

2 cups long grain rice cooked with 3 cups of fish stock (see Bare Necessities)

1 sachet of powdered saffron

2lb (900g) puff pastry (yeast pastry even better)

Handful of chopped parsley and dill

Salt and pepper

6oz (175g) melted butter

Culinary legend would have us believe that Coulibiac is of Russian origin – I am never quite sure about these claims, and know few Russian chefs who may help. Stroganoff at least sounds a bit Russian, and together with coulibiac makes two national dishes which just beats Hungary's solitary claim of goulash. Anyway this is a very good salmon pie.

The salmon fillet should be steamed, poached or cooked in foil for just 10 minutes so that it is barely cooked. Prepare the rice cooked with the fish stock in the usual way. Chop the hard boiled eggs.

Roll the puff pastry into a sheet about ⅛" thick, 12" x 16". On one half of the sheet make a 1" layer of rice, followed by a layer of salmon, followed by chopped egg, followed by salmon, and last another layer of rice. Season well and sprinkle with melted butter and the herbs. Leave a 2" border around the filling to seal the pie. Fold over the pastry sealing the joint with egg wash.

Glaze with egg wash and decorate the top with leaves or pastry fish. Bake for 30 minutes, Gas MK 5 (190C). If pastry is browning too quickly turn down heat or cover with foil.

Serve with a hollandaise sauce (see Bare Necessities) or melted butter. A great cold picnic dish.

BRAISED ORIENTAL GREY MULLET WITH SHITAKE MUSHROOMS

The grey mullet is one of the most under-rated of fish. Very firm flesh makes it ideal for this braising method, and it is an excellent substitute for sea bass. This dish can be as hot as you wish by putting in more or less chilli. Although tempting to cook the fish whole, stick with the fillets as the grey mullet can have a slightly earthy taste when the entire fish is used.

Depending on the size of the fish you will need 8 good sized fillets for 8 people, more if small fish are used.

Keep the coriander and beansprouts aside with the mushrooms.

Place all the remaining ingredients in a flat dish large enough to take the fillets. Lay in the fillets skin side down and braise the fish for about ten minutes depending on size. Remove and keep warm.

Add the fresh coriander and beansprouts to the sauce, heat briefly, and pour over the fish.

Serve the mushrooms on the side.

1 red chilli

1 teaspoon chopped fresh ginger

1 red onion

2 spring onions

2 cloves chopped garlic

2 teaspoons finely chopped lemon grass

1 glass white wine

¼ pint chicken stock (see Bare Necessities)

Salt and pepper

2 tablespoons freshly chopped coriander

2oz (50g) bean sprouts

6oz (150g) shitake mushrooms to sauté in 2oz (50g) very hot butter

BAKER'S WINE SUGGESTION

Grey Mullet is rather overlooked but is, when treated correctly a delicious fish. White Burgundy would be a good match of course but for a change try a quite rare wine from the Loire made from the Chenin Blanc grape. Savenniéres is a tiny appellation and I like to drink Baumard's Clos du Papillon as an aperitif fully to savour its distinctive green apple flavour. This dish requires a little more oomph so look for the top wine of the area M.Joly's Coulée de Serrant. In the old days this wine demanded keeping for over ten years to soften it. However since Nicholas Joly took over from his mother the wine is made bio-dynamically and seems to be ready earlier. The 1990 is very expensive but wonderful – look for the 1991.

HAKE BAKED WITH CHEESE, CIDER AND APPLES

For 8:

8 thick hake portions about 6oz
(175g) each

¼ pint dry cider

¼ pint apple juice

2 eating apples

2oz (50g) butter

8oz (225g) grated mature cheddar

¼ pint double cream

Hake is the national fish dish of Spain, I believe, and this is perhaps some indication that we should pay it more attention. It has a delicate flavour and soft texture which encourages most cooks to serve it on the bone. I actually like to serve a fillet, from a big fish so that it is really succulent. The small fish, so similar to whiting, are best cooked whole. This is a simple family dish rather than one for a dinner party.

Pour the cider and apple juice over the fish, season and bake in the oven for 15 to 20 minutes MK5 (190C) until just firm. Pour the sauce into a wide pan and reduce by half over a high heat. Add the double cream, thicken.

Sauté the apples in the butter. Cover the fillets with the cheese and glaze under a hot grill. Serve with the sauce around the fillets and arrange the apples decoratively.

BAKER'S WINE SUGGESTION

 This needs a subtle white with lots of flavour. There are some excellent Sauvignons being made in New Zealand. Cloudy Bay has the hype but there are plenty of others that have as much quality, Redwood Valley, Hunters, and Wairau River spring to mind.

JOHN DORY STEAMED IN SPINACH WITH LEMON AND CHIVE BUTTER

John Dory or St Pierre (the dark thumb prints on each side of the fish are by legend the marks of St Peter of loaves and fishes fame) is still relatively unknown outside the restaurant circuit – the eyes, the spines and ugly head give no hint of the absolute delicacy of the firm, fine flesh requiring the lightest cooking. Ask your fishmonger to fillet the fish as the spines are quite likely to put you off doing it yourself.

Remove the thick stalky tail of the spinach leaves and blanch the remainder for 30 seconds in salted water, refresh under cold water and lay flat on kitchen paper.

Take the fish fillets and wrap carefully in the leaves overlapping so as to seal in any juices that may come from the fish.

Use a steamer (the woven chinese style are cheap and good) or improvise with a colander or sieve, and steam the fillets for just 7–8 minutes until firm. Whilst you are steaming the fish, reduce the fish stock and white wine by half, add the lemon juice, and rind cut in zests, with the seasoning.

Keeping the sauce swirling, add the butter in knobs until the sauce is smooth. Finally add the chives.

Pour the sauce onto plates, carefully lay the fish on top. The spinach should still be bright green, so try and avoid keeping the fish warm.

For 8 main courses:
4 good sized John Dory
16 good sized spinach leaves
½ pint of fish stock
(see Bare Necessities)
¼ pint of dry white wine
2 tablespoons chopped
fresh chives
4oz (110g) softened butter
Juice and rind of 2 lemons
Seasoning

BAKER'S WINE SUGGESTION

 The Italian wine industry is at last emerging from its lethargy of the last twenty years. Instead of obeying the country's wine laws many of the younger, more progressive wine makers are planting French varieties. The Chardonnay, in the hands of Maurizio Zanella, Gaja or Avignonesi is a marvellously oaky, quite strong wine. Most of the producers are demanding ludicrous prices for their wares but the Il Marzocco of Avignonesi is about a tenner and worth it.

FILLET OF LEMON SOLE WITH CRAB STUFFING AND WATERCRESS SAUCE

For 8 main courses:

16 medium lemon sole fillets

1lb (450g) white crab meat

6 egg whites

¼ pint of fish stock

¼ pint double cream

Parsley and seasoning

For the sauce:

4 bunches of watercress

2 oz (50g) butter melted

¼ pint fish stock

(see Bare Necessities)

¼ pint double cream

Nutmeg, pepper and salt

When sole is mentioned on a menu, unless it states Dover sole it will be the more humble, and much less costly, lemon sole. The two have little in common, and the lemon sole although having a good firm fillet, needs a little help. Hence the crab stuffing here to raise the dish above the every day.

Picking fresh crab is fun but time consuming, but if buying the crab do watch out for freshness – stale crab is horrible as well as potentially hazardous. Brush the fillets with a little cooking oil, lay between two sheets of cooking film and tap out lightly until about twice their original size.

For the stuffing, in a processor blend the crab with the egg whites until stiff. Carefully fold in the cream, beating by hand to a light smooth texture. Season and add the parsley. Chill well.

Spoon a tablespoon of the stuffing near one end of each fillet and roll up. Place in a fairly flat dish, pour over the fish stock and cover with the foil.

For the sauce remove the stalks from the cress and use the leaves only. Liquidise with the melted butter and fish stock, pass through a sieve just before using. Heat the sauce carefully, add the cream, nutmeg and salt and pepper.

To cook the sole, poach gently in preheated oven Gas mark 3 (170C) for 15-20 minutes until firm to the touch.

Serve the sauce on the plate, placing the sole on top, serving any additional sauce separately.

BAKER'S WINE SUGGESTION

Class fish this so try to afford a class white Burgundy from Puligny Montrachet. These wines are the most elegant of the Côte d'Or. Essential, just like with any Burgundy to pick your grower or negotiant with great care. Go for Carillon, Jadot or Joseph Drouhin; the best of them all is probably Sauzet

GRILLED CORNISH MACKEREL WITH PIQUANT RASPBERRY SAUCE

A fresh mackerel takes some beating for flavour, and this crisp fruity sauce is a foil for the rich oiliness of the fish. I suspect that a Cornish fisherman may find this combination somewhat effeminate, but as a variation on the gooseberry theme it is sensational. Raspberry vinegar was one of those cliché ingredients of the eighties but we can't disregard them all! Choose good sized mackerel, very fresh. Ask your fishmonger to fillet the fish.

If you do not have the facility to grill the mackerel, they can be fried. To grill, butter a baking tray or cast-iron dish and grill for 5 minutes skin side up. Try to get the skin browning and crispy with the fish just cooked.

For the sauce reduce the stock with the purée, vinegar and seasoning by half. Add the butter in small pieces, swirling the pan to amalgamate the sauce. Lay the fillets skin-side up on the sauce, decorate with the whole raspberries and chopped parsley.

For 8 you will need:
8 good sized fish – 16 fillets

For the sauce:
½ pint fish stock
(see Bare Necessities)
¼ pint sieved raspberry purée
4 tablespoons raspberry vinegar
3oz (75g) unsalted butter
2 oz whole raspberries
Salt and pepper
Small bunch of parsley

BAKER'S WINE SUGGESTION

Another strong, meaty fish which can well take red wine. Here you need something which tastes like raspberries. Go for a Chinon from the Loire, a red wine from the Cabernet Franc grape. You need to buy a decent vintage of this – the vineyards are a long way North and vintages where there is less sun produce weak, watery wine.

RED MULLET BAKED WITH ORANGE AND ROSEMARY BUTTER

For 8 main courses:

8 fish weighing about

4lb (1.8k) in total

1lb (450g) unsalted butter

8 sprigs rosemary

For the sauce:

½ pint of fresh orange juice

½ pint of dry white wine

4 tablespoons wine vinegar

4oz (110g) unsalted butter

Salt and pepper

3 sprigs of rosemary

The great appeal of the red mullet is the beautiful skin, a reminder of its aphrodisiac qualities – in Roman times greatly prized, and the fresher the fish the redder the skin, so if you eat your mullet the day it's caught, do so for lunch, so better to enjoy the remainder of the day!

Choose fish suitable for one fish per person. Clean and scale the fish, taking care when descaling not to rip the skin.

Arrange each fish in the centre of a piece of foil large enough to enclose it. Fill the cavity with 2oz of sliced butter and a sprig of rosemary, wrap up completely. To cook, bake in a preheated oven MK 3 (170C) for 20 minutes – check it's cooked by the fish eye being white.

Pass the buttery juices from the fish through a sieve. Keep to add to the sauce. While the fish cooks, reduce the orange juice, white wine and vinegar by half with the seasonings and sprigs of rosemary. Pass through a fine sieve, add the fish juice, return to the boil and drop in piece by piece the butter, whisking or swirling the pan to emulsify the sauce. Pour over the fish and serve immediately.

An orange and endive salad is an excellent summer accompaniment.

ROAST COD WITH PINENUT CRUST AND LEMON PEARL BARLEY

Cod has been talked up by the restaurant business no end. My dad was a fish merchant and cod was not a prime fish in our household – far too ordinary! However when really fresh (try and get line-caught inshore cod, that have not been sitting in a fish hold returning from the fishing grounds) it is a succulent, flakey treat and justifies its emergence from the deep fryer. The only salvation when I spent three weeks in the North Atlantic on a trawler, was eating cod cooked immediately it had been landed.

The chef uses cod because it is a great medium for strong sauces and cooking treatments and there is not the inherent problem of being criticised for compromising the flavour as there might be with turbot or sole. Allow about 6oz (175g) of fillet per person, portion individually.

Simmer the barley in the chicken stock, white wine, rind and juice of the lemons and seasoning until tender, about 30 minutes. Add water if getting too thick. Add fresh chopped parsley and fresh thyme.

Place the cod on a baking sheet in a hot oven MK 7 (220C) for about 15 minutes depending on the thickness of the fillets; watch the crust does not burn. The centre of the fish should be only just cooked, even slightly under if possible.

Serve on the barley with extra lemon zest and parsley.

Even my dad might have been convinced!

8 thick cod fillets
For the crust:
3oz (75g) crushed pinenuts
3oz (75g) chopped parsley
Enough olive oil to bind into thick paste. Season and spread over the fillets.

Lemon pearl barley
8oz (225g) pearl barley
¼ pint chicken stock
¼ pint white wine
Rind and juice of 2 lemons
Seasoning
Tablespoon fresh parsley and thyme

BAKER'S WINE SUGGESTION

Firm fleshed fish deserves a firm fleshed wine. Try something from Italy with a lot of interest like vintage Tunina from Jermann. This is the premium wine from that producer and is a blend. A curious wine, difficult to find and expensive, c. £20 a bottle. Still if you drink white Burgundy with fish…

SPICED MONKFISH WITH SAFFRON RICE

For 8 main courses:

1½lb (675g) trimmed monkfish tail

1 clove chopped garlic

2 tablespoons lemon juice

Coffeespoon salt

2 tablespoons olive oil

½ tablespoon of each of the following: cumin, coriander, cardamom, cayenne, curry powder.

4 tablespoons clarified butter to sauté the fish

Saffron rice:

1 shallot

2oz (50g) butter

6oz (175g) long grain rice

1 pint water

1 sachet powdered saffron

Putting together these recipes from the chaotically organised grease – stained kitchen notes of many years, it has been apparent how strong a penchant we have had for spiced dishes. I am not sure why, in that I do not have to my knowledge a Moroccan grandmother, and have not travelled extensively in the Middle East.

I suspect that the restaurant chef is eager to make a positive impression, with memorable flavours, to avoid rich sauces and thus seeks help from the spices and aromas of other cuisines. Many have been similarly inspired by dishes from Japan and Thailand.

Make a marinade of all the spices, lemon, oil and garlic. Slice the fish into ¼" rounds and thoroughly mix with the spiced marinade. Leave for at least three hours.

For the Saffron Rice finely chop a shallot or half onion. Soften in butter, add rice, and mix well with the butter. Add water, saffron and season. Simmer with a lid partially off, for fifteen minutes. Stand with lid on for ten minutes.

To cook the fish, preheat a sauté pan and sauté the fish for about five minutes in clarified butter, depending on the size of the pieces. Sprinkle with fresh coriander and with all the juices serve on top of the rice.

BAKER'S WINE SUGGESTION

Monkfish is the meatiest of all white fish. There are recipes for big Monk tails that cook it like a 'gigot', others use port sauce. You are talking of chunky food here and you need chunky wine. Miguel Torres makes a delicious but expensive oaky Chardonnay in Penedes, Spain. It is called Milmanda and would accompany this dish brilliantly. If you can't get that try a good white Burgundy or Chardonnay from Italy, South Africa or even Australia, although their wines may be too heavy for this dish.

POULTRY AND GAME

We have always had excellent game in Britain and now we also have quality domestic poultry. Free-range and maize-fed chickens, Gressingham ducks, guinea fowl or turkey (sometimes) are now produced by farmers who care for flavour over profit, although there is still an approach from the frozen front that prices chicken at less than dog food. You get what you pay for as they say. The white meat revolution encouraged by the health fads and beef scares has made poultry a number one best seller. The game bird is probably the most perfect example of non-intensive free-range rearing that is possible; nurtured on grain, turned out into fields and woodland to forage naturally, and hung 'in the feather', this is poultry perfection. Take advantage of the harvest from fieldsports, as the guns are paying all the costs!

Game birds and venison need some care in their cooking as they have little fat and can therefore be dry. The breast of a game bird requires very little cooking and it is often worth removing them from the carcass, allowing the legs to continue cooking; very underdone grouse is not to everyone's taste, but it is a crime to overcook such a prized delicacy. The humble pigeon breast can be delectable and the whole bird can be braised slowly to great effect. In the restaurant we serve chicken in a hundred different ways and how difficult to choose a few for a recipe book. The intention is to demonstrate a method, which with different ingredients will allow many variants on the theme. There is no apology for including a version of coq au vin, since it is the introduction to all composite braising dishes, and one day soon there will be a generation of restaurant goers who have never had it before!

COQ AU VIN WITH GRATIN DAUPHINOIS POTATOES

Virtually my first task in the kitchen as a young commis at Kenneth Bell's famous Thornbury Castle in 1970, was to tackle Elizabeth David's Coq au vin de Bourgogne from French Provincial Cooking. I think it took me all day, but it remains a great favourite, despite the abuse the dish has received at the hands of the boil-in-the-bag merchants.

You need a good sized boiling chicken so that the flesh holds together, the legs being the best part.

For eight people:

2 medium chickens, jointed on the bone

1½ bottles of full bodied red wine (Rhône is better than Burgundy)

½ pint chicken stock (see Bare Necessities)

2 onions

6 cloves garlic

4 streaky rashers bacon

Bouquet garni of thyme, bay and rosemary

2 tablespoons brown sugar

4oz (110g) small button onions

4oz (110g) small mushrooms

4oz (110g) plain flour

8 tablespoons olive oil

Seasoning

4oz (110g) white grapes

In a heavy-bottomed pan large enough to cook the whole dish, heat half the oil. Lay the chicken skin down to cover the base of the pan. Brown well, briefly turn over, remove to a tray and repeat with the remaining pieces, adding the remaining oil as necessary.

Reduce the heat, add the chopped bacon, onion, garlic, sugar and seasoning and fry until beginning to colour. Replace the chicken, legs first, breasts on top, sprinkle over the flour shaking the pan vigorously.

Add the wine, stock and bouquet garni with the button onions. Simmer gently for 15 minutes, remove the breast portions, simmer for another 20-30 minutes and remove leg portions.

Reduce the sauce by at least ⅓ adding the mushrooms for the last 5 minutes. The sauce should be shiny and rich but not overthick. Pour over the chicken, decorate with triangles of fried bread and halved grapes.

BAKER'S WINE SUGGESTION

It has to be Burgundy of course. In these days where Colonels do not really believe that what is in a Burgundy bottle is what they were used to in the past, we all look to really good producers to give us the taste and flavour of the Pinot Noir, that notoriously difficult to grow variety. Keep bigger wines for bigger dishes and go for a Savigny (the best men are Bise and Ampeau) a Pernand Vergelesses or an Auxey Duresses. These will neither break the bank nor overpower the Chicken.

For eight:

Slice 4lb (1.8K) potatoes
into thin slices (50p thick!)
1 clove garlic
1pt double cream
¼ pint milk

Anyone who has eaten at our restaurants will be familiar with the potato dish known as Gratin Dauphinois, just the right accompaniment to Coq au vin. This is the simple way:

Dry the potatoes thoroughly with kitchen paper.

Chop a clove of garlic and spread in the base of a gratin dish.

Layer the potatoes, season well. Mix 1 pint double cream with ¼ pint milk and pour over the potatoes; they should now be just covered.

Bake for 1½ hours, Mk 2 150C, until well browned.
Keep warm in low oven.

BLANQUETTE OF WILD RABBIT

For 8 main courses:

4 medium rabbits
6oz (175g) flour
4oz (110g) butter
4 rashers streaky bacon
2 carrots, sliced
2 dozen pickling onions (if
unavailable slice two large onions)
4 cloves garlic
1 medium leek
Handful chopped tarragon
(put the stalks into the stew)
1 bottle dry white wine
½ pint double cream
3 egg yolks

A classic dish which we have always enjoyed doing is the Blanquette de veau. Veal is, however, not as much in demand as it was and rabbit is very much on the return so rabbit gets the vote. The real reason that this is more than just another stew is the use of a 'liaison'; this is not unfortunately an invitation to a diversion of the 'dangerous' type but thickening of the broth with a little egg yolk to make a light velvety sauce.

There are wild rabbits for sale and bred ones. I assume that wild have more flavour but have to admit that we ate the best rabbit ever in Italy where the restaurant owner told us that they bred their own rabbits and the secret was the age. Mature but not old, which makes sense. Perhaps the best request that could be made of the butcher would be for wild but not too large animals.

Assuming a back leg and half a saddle as a generous portion, you will need four rabbits for eight people with the front legs as a bonus. Ask the butcher to joint them for you.

Roll the jointed meat in the flour and brown quickly in the hot butter. Remove and fry the bacon. Put back the rabbit, legs at the bottom, and add the vegetables, seasoning and wine.

Simmer for fifteen minutes and remove the saddles. Cook the legs for a further fifteen minutes. Use some judgement here as to the size and age of the rabbit since it is a myth that rabbit should be cooked for hours! At this stage the dish can be set aside until ready for serving or kept in the fridge overnight.

When ready to serve, heat the stew but do not cook for any length of time. Pour the liquid through a sieve into a bowl.

Whisk the cream and yolks with the fresh tarragon, pour on the cooking liquid, whisk well. In a separate pan bring this sauce carefully up to temperature, but do not boil.

Place the rabbit and vegetables on plates and spoon over the sauce.

Some additional baby vegetables could be added to provide colour. Serve with creamy mashed potato.

BAKER'S WINE SUGGESTION

 Rabbit is essentially a peasant dish and a good French Country Wine would be ideal here. It must clearly not be too huge a wine but yet must have good sweetness and fruitiness. The Domaines Virginie outside Beziers make outstanding white and red wines which are widely available in the market. This rabbit really needs a light red and their Merlot would do well. If you cannot find wines from Virginie then look around for other Pays d'Oc Merlot but beware some are much better than others – at least at the price one can afford to experiment.

PHEASANT POT-ROASTED WITH SAVOY CABBAGE AND SMOKED BACON

For 8 you will need:

4 pheasants

2 savoy cabbages

2 onions

4 cloves garlic

4 rashers smoked thick cut bacon

¼ bottle dry white wine

4 oz (110g) butter

Bunch of thyme

I suppose that it is likely that at some time in the early part of the next century game shooting will be banned in this country. No doubt pheasant would then be reared in much the same way that we now take for granted with guinea-fowl or quail. I am sure the bird will no longer be as flavoursome as those that now freely roam the countryside and of course they will become an expensive luxury. Enjoy them while you can!

Be wary of the inherent difficulty of cooking pheasant; it is a dry bird, old pheasants are leathery, over-cooked, old pheasants are appalling! This recipe is designed to make the best of a tricky bird.

In a generous heavy-bottomed pan, heat the butter and brown the pheasants all over. Remove and put aside. Reduce the heat, add the diced bacon, fry until crisp, then add the onion and garlic and allow to colour lightly.

Put back the pheasants, add the cabbage, shredded, the white wine and thyme. Simmer, preferably in the oven for approximately 45 minutes (MK 3, 170C) depending on the size of the birds (see above). To serve, spoon the moist cabbage onto plates, remove the pheasant breasts and legs and serve one of each.

Add a little stock or water if the dish is looking dry while cooking.

BAKER'S WINE SUGGESTION

Pheasant needs hanging really well these days as most of them are fed on maize until they meet their early demise and taste of very little. Assume that you have a proper, tasty one and go to the Rhône again for a big, fruity wine. Côte Rôtie would be ideal, the clean Syrah flavour seems well suited to pheasant. The best wines come from Guigal, Ogier Rostaing.

DUCK BREAST AND STUFFED LEG WITH LENTILS, BACON AND GARLIC

There is a hint of the great dish Cassoulet from south-west France here. The lentils make for a lighter sauce than beans, but still have that property of absorbing any fattiness from the duck. Try the Puy lentils which are small. Ducks are now available in all sorts of guises. The advantage of the newer varieties is that they have less fat, and being crosses between wild and domestic birds, have excellent flavour.

Remove the legs and breasts from the duck. Remove the leg bones and tap out the flesh until flat (best done between sheets of cling film).

To make the stuffing, sweat the finely chopped onions and mushrooms in the butter, add the egg and breadcrumbs and bind with the seasoning and orange juice.

Wrap the leg meat around the stuffing to make eight stuffed legs. Tie if necessary or secure with cocktail sticks. Roast legs slowly to cook through, about 30 minutes Gas Mk 4 (180C).

Lentils should be soaked overnight and rinsed. Sauté the diced bacon and chopped garlic, add stock and lentils and cook for 15 to 20 minutes (different types take more or less time). Finish by adding cream.

Now roast the duck breasts in a hot oven MK7 (220C) for 20 minutes, and allow to rest in a warm place for a further 10. Put the lentil sauce on the plates, slice the pink duck breasts and stuffed legs and arrange decoratively over the sauce. Sprinkle with fresh thyme and parsley.

You will need for 8 people:

4 small duck (Gressingham or Barbary are good)

The stuffing for the legs:

4 onions

4oz (110g) mushrooms

Rind and juice of 2 oranges

6oz (175g) brown breadcrumbs

2 eggs

4oz (110g) butter

Salt, pepper, thyme and basil

The sauce:

1lb mixed brown and green lentils

2 rashers bacon

2 cloves garlic

1 pint veal stock

(see Bare Necessities)

½ pint double cream

Parsley for decoration

BAKER'S WINE SUGGESTION

 In Harry's Bar in Venice they serve a wine called Venegazzu. They charge about £20 for it. As the wine is made about forty miles away this seems a little excessive as you can buy it over here for about a tenner. It is made from Bordeaux grapes, the Cabernet, Cabernet Franc and Merlot. Plenty of spice and body to partner this pulsey dish.

BREAST OF GUINEA-FOWL BAKED IN PASTRY WITH PIQUANT FRESH LIMES AND ORANGE

You will need for 8 people:

4 guinea-fowl

2 onions

4oz (110g) mushrooms

Rind and juice of 4 limes,

2 oranges

1 extra orange and lime for
segments

4oz (110g) butter

1lb (450g) puff pastry

(see Bare Necessities or buy in)

½ bottle dry white wine

½ pint chicken stock

(see Bare Necessities)

Teaspoon fresh thyme
and rosemary

Seasoning

2 tablespoons chopped parsley

Guinea-fowl is just the kind of meat we should be using, not intensively reared, more flavour than chicken with less fat. Perhaps closer to pheasant but less gamey, less dry and less full of shot! This recipe is a little bit grand and just uses the breast, but keep the legs for another dish, or incorporate them into the stock for extra flavour.

Remove the breasts from the guinea-fowl without bone, set the legs aside for another dish or leave on the carcass for the stock. Put the carcasses in a generous pot with roughly chopped carrot, onion, parsley stalks etc for a stock which should simmer for about an hour until reduced and concentrated.

Make a 'duxelles' by finely chopping the onion and mushroom and cooking in half of the butter with half of the orange and lime juices, herbs and seasoning until soft and quite dry. Chill.

In the remaining butter, sauté the breasts until just firm and lightly browned but not cooked. Cool and make a short incision down the side and fill each breast with the duxelles. Chill.

Roll out the pastry into a sheet about ¼" thick and cut into long strips about ¼" wide. Carefully coil around the breasts, slightly overlapping as though one was bandaging the guinea-fowl. Chill.

For the sauce, reduce the white wine and stock to half a pint. Add the zests of lime and orange. Season. At the last minute put in the segments of remaining fruit and the chopped parsley.

To cook, glaze the pastry with eggwash, bake the guinea-fowl in a preheated hot oven for 25 minutes gas MK 6 (200C). Watch the pastry doesn't catch.

BAKER'S WINE SUGGESTION

White wine would probably suit this well but it would have to be one with considerably flavour and interest. One of the new style White Bordeaux like Ch Couhins Lurton or de Fieuzal (or better still Ygrec, the dry white of Yquem) have the Semillon punch to carry this dish.

SAUTE OF FREE-RANGE CHICKEN WITH APPLE AND CALVADOS

A classic Normandy dish, perhaps not so PC these days because of the cream, but one of the great chicken dishes to be enjoyed occasionally. If a roast chicken is preferred the sauce can be completed in a roasting pan in similar fashion, but the chicken will not be cooking in the sauce so will not have the intensity of flavour of the original.

The chicken should be jointed on the bone to allow a half breast plus thigh or drumstick per person.

Heat 1oz (25g) of the clarified butter and brown the chicken, skin side down, keeping the temperature high not allowing the chicken to stew in its own liquid. You will need a second 1oz of butter during this process.

Pour off surplus fat, put the chicken back in the pan, add apple juice, shallots and seasoning and simmer for fifteen minutes before removing the breasts, and a further ten before removing the legs. Reduce the remaining sauce by half.

Meanwhile segment the apples and fry in the remaining butter.

Remove the chicken to a serving dish.

Add the cream to the sauce and boil briskly to a smooth consistency. Ensure the chicken is in a dish that will stand the heat, pour over the Calvados, flame it, pour the sauce around and arrange the apple slices decoratively.

For 8 you will need:

2 medium free-range chickens

1 pint fresh apple juice

4 chopped shallots

4oz (110g) clarified butter

½ pint double cream

8 tablespoons calvados

6 Cox's apples

Seasoning

BAKER'S WINE SUGGESTION

A real Norman dish here and one that is very difficult to put with wine. I suggest a good bottle of strong West country or Normandy cider. If you don't like this idea try a white wine with some sweetness and richness, Vouvray can work here; Hurt makes the finest.

STEAMED BREAST OF MARINATED FREE-RANGE CHICKEN WITH LEMON, GARLIC, MINT AND YOGURT.

For 8 you will need:

8 breasts of free-range chicken

Rind and juice of 3 lemons

2 cloves garlic

Handful chopped mint

and parsley

6oz (175g) greek thick yogurt

½ pint chicken stock

½ pint dry white wine

Seasonings

A simple dish with a hint of Greece as well as healthy modernity. A perfect summer dish. If there is no steamer available wrap the breasts in foil with a little olive oil and bake in preheated oven for 30 minutes, Mk 5 (190C)

24 hours before cooking the dish, prepare the marinade.

Remove the skin from the chicken breast.

In a sufficiently deep-sided container cover the breasts with the zests and juice of the lemons, wine, finely chopped garlic, mint and stock.

Turn the breasts over once during marinating.

To cook, pass off the marinade, which will be the sauce, into a saucepan and reduce the liquid by half. Steam the breasts in a steamer for about 15 minutes.

To finish the sauce add the yogurt off the boil, whisk well and add some fresh mint and parsley.

Spoon on to plates, slice the chicken breasts and lay on the sauce.

Decorate with more lemon zests.

Serve with an interesting rice – basmati or risotto.

BAKER'S WINE SUGGESTION

 An opportunity here to serve a really spicy Gewurztraminer, which in addition to going well with dishes like this can be the only wine which remotely suits Chinese and Indian food. Go for a producer of note, Hugel, Trimbach, Deissar, Schlumberger and avoid the insipid wines of the co-operatives.

ROAST SADDLE OF HARE WITH GREEN NOODLES AND WILD MUSHROOMS

Hare is something of a 'bloody' challenge for the cook. I do not consider myself squeamish, but prefer these days to order my hare jointed from the butcher. For this dish we are using just the saddle, sometimes available on their own but if not the remainder of the hare is left for a wonderful civet!

Remove the fine membrane from the hare with a sharp pointed knife, wrap in streaky bacon and roast with bay leaf and rosemary for 30 minutes in hot oven MK6 (200C). Remove and allow to rest.

Reduce the stock and wine by half, add the jelly and Madeira and the mushrooms (if using dried they will need to be soaked and washed first).

To complete the sauce swirl in the butter at the last minute. Carefully fillet the saddles just as though filleting a fish; slice the fillets and arrange decoratively on the sauce.

Boil the noodles for just two minutes, toss in olive oil and arrange on the plate.

For eight portions:

The saddle of two large hares

8 rashers streaky bacon

8 bay leafs

8 sprigs rosemary

For the green noodles:

See recipe for shellfish with spinach pasta (pg 46) or buy fresh noodles

For the sauce:

½ pint veal stock
(see Bare Necessities)

¼ pint red wine

¼ pint Madeira

2 tablespoons redcurrant jelly

6oz (175g) mushrooms – some dried wild type such as porcini or morels would be best

2oz (50g) softened butter

BAKER'S WINE SUGGESTION

Hare is another very gamey flavour and I still think the best wines for this are from the Rhône. Try a Hermitage or Crozes Hermitage of real quality. Hermitage la Chapelle from Jaboulet or Hermitage from Chave. Crozes from Graillot, Jaboulet or Chapoutier all produce marvellous peppery wines.

ROAST WOOD PIGEON WITH GARLIC CREAM SAUCE

For 8 you will need:

16 plump pigeon breasts

8oz (225g) butter

½ pint chicken stock

8 cloves garlic

¼ pint double cream

¼ pint dry white wine

Fresh parsley

Seasoning

Many restaurants now choose to use the more extravagantly reared squabs for the table, but the humble wood pigeon has plenty of flavour. The breasts must be lightly cooked. The alternative is to braise the bird slowly so it is succulent and falling off the bone. For entertaining I suggest using just the breasts and using the remainder for a game soup. Most butchers will also sell the breast only.

Prepare the sauce in advance, which reheats very easily.

Peel the garlic and blanch in salted water 10 minutes, changing the water twice. Blend the blanched garlic with the chicken stock and pass through a fine sieve. Reduce this flavoured stock with the wine and seasoning, add the cream and chopped parsley; continue to reduce until a rich texture is achieved.

Butter the breasts and roast in a hot oven MK7 (220C) for 15 minutes, longer if less pinkness required. Leave to rest for 15 minutes.

Arrange decoratively sliced over the sauce with a sauté of mushrooms and saffron rice (pg 78).

BAKER'S WINE SUGGESTION

Although the garlic is not strong (having been cooked) in this dish, the flavour of it is. A good strong red from the south of France would go well here. Several villages and producers are worth seeking out. The Bandol of Domaine des Tempiers or Mas de la Rouviere (Bunan); Mas du Daumas Gassac a Cabernet based wine of some distinction but an outrageous price, or go to the South West of France and try a blockbuster wine like Madiran.

ROAST HAUNCH OF ROE DEER WITH COMPOTE OF RED ONIONS IN RED WINE

For many years our venison was supplied to us by a country poacher who taught us a good deal about the merits of different types of venison. Unfortunately the law did not always agree with his traditional methods and the early morning visits in the battered Land Rover ceased. We had however acquired a feel for using this lovely dark meat.

There is often a misconception that venison is a tough, dry meat that needs days of marinating and hours of cooking. Roe or fallow, particularly younger animals, produce a haunch quite similar to a leg of lamb with much less fat and a flavour close to beef. The leg requires some protection from dryness by using bacon, pork fat or foil during the cooking. This has to be the best alternative for those nervous of beef.

The haunch is more easily handled, cooked and carved if boned in advance, with the bacon tied around the joint. Roast with the butter for 1 hour Gas Mark 5 (190C) or about 15 minutes to the pound. Allow the meat to rest for at least 15 minutes before serving.

For the compôte, fry the finely sliced onions in the butter. Add the remaining ingredients and simmer for an hour until the compôte reaches a texture reminiscent of runny marmalade. Slice the venison adding any juices to the onions.

Excellent with gratin dauphinois (see pg 82).

A small to medium haunch will feed 8 people.

For roasting:
6oz (175g) smoked streaky bacon
Bunch thyme and rosemary
2oz (50g) butter

Red onion compôte:
10 red onions
2oz (50g) butter
½ bottle red wine
2 tablespoons redcurrant jelly
1 tablespoon brown sugar
Seasoning

BAKER'S WINE SUGGESTION

Venison demands very chunky wine. About the chunkiest are the wines of Piedmont in northern Italy. In the old days these wines were often kept too long in oak making them liable to oxidisation; the good thing is that many of the producers have now made a conscious decision to make lighter wines for early consumption. Go for Sito Morsco or Vignaveja from Gaja or Nebbiolo delle Langhe from Mascarello.

91

ROAST GROUSE WITH PIQUANT PORT AND CRANBERRY SAUCE

For eight people you will need:

8 young grouse

8 rashers of back bacon

8oz (225g) butter

8 slices toast

For the sauce:

1 pint veal stock
(see Bare Necessities)

1lb (450g) cranberries

¼ pint port

¼ pint red wine

4 tablespoons raspberry vinegar

2 tablespoons brown sugar

Seasoning

The opportunities to enjoy grouse are few. The season is short, prices are high, but to me this is the pick of the game bird bag and worth the extravagance.

The first requirement is to get involved in the hanging of the birds. Too often the butcher will dress the grouse before it has been hung sufficiently. The hanging depends on the weather, but about 4-5 days in a cool place is ample.

This is a powerful sauce that also goes well with hare or venison.

Cover the breasts of the grouse with the bacon, spread with the softened butter and place in a roasting tray and roast for about 30 minutes, Mk 6 (200C). The time depends on taste, but keep the breast pink and put the legs back to cook further if necessary.

While the birds are roasting reduce the stock, wine and vinegar and seasonings by half.

Add the port and sugar and, only at the last minute, the cranberries.

Remove the breasts and legs and lay on the slices of toast (the traditional method is to spread the livers of the birds on the toast).

Spoon the sauce around the grouse.

BAKER'S WINE SUGGESTION

Grouse is the strongest of all game that is worth eating and carries port and Cranberries well. The combination has strength and sweetness so go to the Southern Rhône. Find a good mature Châteauneuf du Pape from Beaucastel or Vieux Telegraphe. If you want to carry on the theme of Cranberries try a Zinfandel. This is immensely strong and, when mature, can be as good as Rhône with game dishes.

BEEF AND LAMB

At the height of the BSE scare we took beef off our menu at the Olive Tree because we thought it would not sell. Within a week by popular demand it was back. Beef is a central mainstream dish that is part of our culture and is bound to remain so. Offal which has never been so enthusiastically embraced may cease to be part of such culinary lore, as the vegetarian teenager of today is likely to be the household cook of tomorrow. The beef recipes here use generally fine cuts, which are popular restaurant dishes but all those of us who cook for pleasure as well as gain, perhaps prefer to spend time also on the less glamourous and cheaper joints.

Lamb is a much more straightforward pleasure. Whether an aromatic stew or a succulent best end in Spring, the meat is the cook's best friend; easy to prepare and so tolerant of inattention. Even the French accept our lamb to be the world's best and from Wales to the salt marshes of Romney, they hunt it out and push up the price!

A rather horrified young kitchen assistant commented, on seeing pink lamb being carved, that her mother had always said that a leg of lamb should be left in the oven overnight to be cooked right through. Well personal preference is all, but do serve roast lamb lightly cooked and avoid a slow and lingering death of a wonderful meat!

BRAISED BEEF SKIRT WITH ELDERBERRY VINEGAR

We have many years of happy association with the Pitt family. Both brothers, Rupert and Antony, have worked with us in our kitchens and are artistic and sensitive chefs. It was Rupert who introduced me to elderberry vinegar, and while I may have had some suspicions of his home-made wine, his vinegar is sensational.

Elderberries being free and plentiful are a wild harvest not to be missed. The choice of the beef skirt, or blade steak as an alternative, is for that long, coarse grain which, when well cooked flakes and can nearly be eaten with a spoon.

Ask your butcher to prepare you eight pieces of skirt, quite thick, 6-8oz (200g) They should be trimmed of sinew but some fat will help the cooking.

Dust the steaks in the flour and brown in the hot butter. Remove. Add the shallots and garlic, cook for a few minutes. Put back the meat, add the remaining ingredients and simmer for about two hours. If the stew is looking short of liquid add a little water.

Serve with some additional elderberries sprinkled over the top if you have them, and with coarsely chopped flat-leaf parsley.

Elderberry vinegar:

The longer this keeps the better, so during September when the berries are plentiful make as much as possible.

Cover 1lb (450g) elderberries with 1¾ pints of white wine vinegar. Leave for twenty-four hours. Strain this liquid over a second 1lb of berries the next day and leave to stand again. Strain carefully, add 6oz white sugar, bring to boil to dissolve sugar. Pass through muslin to strain and bottle in old wine bottles that have been carefully washed. Cork and keep for at least a month before using.

8 beef skirt steaks 6-8oz (200g) each

4oz (110g) butter

4oz (110g) flour

6 shallots, finely chopped

3 cloves garlic, finely chopped

¼ pint elderberry vinegar (see below). Use sherry vinegar or part wine, part raspberry vinegar, if the time of year is wrong.

½ pint veal stock (see Bare Necessities)

¼ pint red wine

Thyme, bay and rosemary

Seasoning

Chopped flat-leaf parsley to finish the dish

BAKER'S WINE SUGGESTION

A powerful dish with quite a bit of acidity needing a wine without a lot. Although Claret is usually my preferred glass with beef I would move to burgundy with this stew. The elderberry flavour will work well with a youngish Pinot Noir. Burgundy these days is much misunderstood, many of the wines are not deep in colour but still deliver the goods (some however are weak and weedy due to the greed of the vignerons concerned). For this dish look for a Côte Chalonnaise wine from Rully, Mercurey or Givry. The Mercureys of Faiveley and Ch de Merley are of requisite quality and depth.

RACK OR BEST END OF LAMB WITH MINT CRUST AND SAUCE OF SHALLOTS AND MINT

For 8:

4 single best ends of lamb

Finely chopped small onion

Finely chopped clove garlic

3oz (75g) butter

8oz (225g) breadcrumbs

4 tablespoons chopped mint

2 eggs

1 tablespoon dijon mustard

For the sauce:

½ pint of veal or lamb stock

(see Bare Necessities)

¼ pint red wine

4 shallots finely chopped

Handful chopped mint

4 tablespoons sherry vinegar

1 tablespoon redcurrant jelly

Seasoning

2oz (50g) softened butter

The best end of neck of lamb sounds less glamorous than the rack, but it's the same thing and a very convenient, posh little joint for small numbers, and cooks quickly, hence so often seen in restaurants. Make sure your butcher chines and trims the joint neatly so that it looks decorative with the tops of the bones scraped clean and most of the fat removed.

For 8 people you will need 4 single best ends of lamb to give 3 chops each.

Soften the onion and clove of chopped garlic in the butter. In a processor make the breadcrumbs and blend in the chopped fresh mint. Mix the onion with the crumbs and the 2 eggs to bind the mixture. Score the joints with the point of a sharp knife, spread with the Dijon mustard and then the mixture on top.

Reduce the stock by half, with wine and shallots. Add the vinegar, seasoning and redcurrant jelly. At the last minute, add the butter in small knobs and finish with the fresh mint.

Roast the joints for 20 – 25 minutes Mk 6 (200C), leave to rest for 10 minutes. Cut into chops being careful with the crust and lay the chops on the sauce.

BAKER'S WINE SUGGESTION

Good Claret always partners Lamb best for me. A really fruity St Julien or Pauillac from a drinkable vintage (like 1985, 1983, 1981, 1979 or 1970) would be ideal. If you want to go further afield find a good Australian or Californian Cabernet

BEEF RUMP WITH ARMAGNAC AND MUSCAT GRAPES

Rump is not as fashionable as it once was – perhaps because as a cut it's more complicated to handle than sirloin or fillet, but for flavour it is the best of all.

This is a braised dish – the secret being slow cooking. One can either cook and serve the whole piece or cut into chunks – the latter cooking more quickly. If you are going to serve a whole piece ask the butcher for a good thick bit from the 'point' end, rather than a long, thin, steak-thickness piece.

Marinate the halved grapes in the Armagnac.

In a large pan heat the oil until smoking and brown the meat all over. Remove from the pan.

Lower the heat, add the bacon, onions and garlic, seasoning. Continue to cook for five minutes. Stir in the flour and allow to colour. Put back the meat, add the liquids (not the grapes) and herbs and simmer for 2 hours depending on the size of the joint, (1 hour if the meat is cut into chunks). 20 minutes before serving add the mushrooms and grapes. If the sauce is too liquid remove the meat and reduce the sauce.

For 8:

3-4lb (1.5 k) rump

2 large onions, roughly chopped

2 rashers smoked bacon

4 cloves garlic chopped

8oz (225g) button mushrooms

1 bottle red wine

6oz (175g) plain flour

4 tablespoons cooking oil

½ pint veal stock

(see Bare Necessities)

8oz (225g) Muscat grapes

seeded and skinned

¼ pint of Armagnac!

Bundle of rosemary and thyme

Seasoning

BAKER'S WINE SUGGESTION

The ideal place to drink one of the new 'Super Tuscan' wines. Many are following the lead of Antinori's Tignanello and making wines from the native grapes with the addition of Cabernet Sauvignon. Some notable producers are Ca del' Pazzo, Carmignano, Castello di Volpaia, Monte Vertine and Avignonesi. These have huge fruit and weight – well worth a try.

For 8:

1 whole shoulder lamb, boned, trimmed and cut up into good sized chunks about 2" square

2 cloves garlic

2 rashers bacon

1 onion peeled and 'stuck' with about 20 cloves

1 onion chopped

1 bottle red wine

2 tablespoons sultanas

1 tablespoon brown sugar

1 tablespoon ground cinnamon

Salt & pepper

4 tablespoons olive oil

Why such a culinarily conservative population as ours so much enjoys spiced food is curious. Some echo of a colonial past, some reaction against the subtlety of French cuisine, who knows but our restaurant dishes with a hint of the Orient have always been among the most popular. This dish is about sweet scented spice not hot aggressive spice.

Heat the oil until smoking and brown the lamb pieces, not too many at a time and remove to one side. Turn down the heat, add the bacon, chopped onion, garlic finely chopped, and allow to colour. Add the spices and sugar and cook for a further five minutes. Put back the meat, add the clove onion, cover with the wine and slowly simmer for 1 hour until tender (In the oven Mk 2 150C). Fifteen minutes before serving add the sultanas.

Serve with basmati rice and spiced okra or sesame-flavoured cabbage.

BAKER'S WINE SUGGESTION

Light Pinot Noir wine would go well with this dish. Chorey les Beaune from Tollot Beaut or a Ladoix from Drouhin perhaps. Or be adventurous and try one of the increasingly good Californian Pinots like Au Bon Climat or Saintsbury. From that continent perhaps the most successful Pinots are from Oregon - Domain or Ponzi

LEG OF LAMB BRAISED IN RED WINE WITH ORANGES AND ROSEMARY

It must be a quirky cook that gets more pleasure from the preparation of a dish than from its consumption, but this wonderfully aromatic stew is such a treat to have simmering in the oven, filling the kitchen with Mediterranean sunshine that the pleasure of its eating is probably surpassed by the intoxication of first lifting the lid!

The day before, cover the lamb with the red wine, herbs, rind and juice of the oranges, to marinate for about 12 hours.

In a generous stew pan, heat the olive oil, dry the meat on kitchen paper and sauté a little at a time until brown, turning frequently. When all the meat is removed add the bacon, chopped onions and garlic, and colour. A little extra olive oil may need to be added. Put back the meat, sprinkle with flour, shake the pan to distribute the flour, add the marinade and seasoning and simmer for about an hour in the oven, Gas MK 3,170C. Test a piece of meat which should be very tender.

Meanwhile, blanch and refresh the baby vegetables.

Serve with orange zest and the reheated baby vegetables.

For 8:

1 leg of lamb boned and trimmed, cut into chunks about 3" square

Bottle of full red wine

4 rashers streaky bacon

2 onions

4 cloves garlic

4 oranges

Thyme, rosemary and bay tied in a muslin bundle

4 tablespoons flour

4 tablespoons olive oil

Decorative vegetables to serve as a garnish such as baby carrots, turnips, mange tout, broad beans.

BAKER'S WINE SUGGESTION

 This needs something more exotic than Bordeaux really but you could try a very rich Pomerol. Otherwise a lighter wine from the Syrah grape; Qupé makes a particularly good one which is real value for money in Southern California. St Joseph or a Côtes du Rhône would also fit the bill.

OSSO BUCO – SHIN OF VEAL BRAISED WITH TOMATOES, LEMON AND WINE

For 8:

(8 slices shin of veal about 2" thick)

4oz (110g) butter

1 pint white wine

4lb (1.7k) chopped tomato (tinned is fine)

2 cloves garlic

2 medium onions

Rind and juice of 2 lemons

Seasoning

Gremolata to sprinkle over the finished dish (see loin of pork recipe pg109)

Perhaps we should be really calling this Ossi Buchi as there are several slices of the shin. Veal is, of course, absolutely central to Italian cooking, and this traditional Milanese dish has always been a great favourite. The obsession of the restaurant trade with all things Italian has been selective in disregarding most of the veal dishes which I suspect an Italian may feel is most curious.

Ask your butcher to cut 8 slices of shin about 2" thick. He or she may need persuading to give you pieces that all the same size, so you may need an extra slice or two if the lower pieces of shin are too small.

Heat the butter in a large stew pan and brown the veal slices. Remove. Add the chopped onion and garlic, cook for a few minutes and return the meat with the tomatoes and wine, the lemon rind and juice.

Simmer gently for about 1½ hours. Remove the meat and reduce the sauce if you feel that it is too thin.

The skin around the slices of veal can be removed at this stage for a little refinement but do leave the bone in the middle as this is part of the presentation of the dish.

Put the sauce over the meat and sprinkle with the gremolata.

A risotto would be appropriate with this or mashed potatoes with olive oil.

BAKER'S WINE SUGGESTION

 Angelo Gaja is the king of Piedmontese (and probably Italian) winemakers. His prices reflect this position, his single vineyard Barbarescos fetch over fifty pounds a bottle. This tends to frighten off British consumers. Gaja does have a string of less expensive wines which are made with equal care and reflect his passion for fruit and flavour. A dish like Osso buco demands a smooth and yet assertive red wine and Gaja's simple Nebbiolo delle Langhe would suit well. The name of the wine is Vignaveja. In great vintages it needs about ten years to be ready to drink so look for a lesser vintage such as 1991.

BEEF FILLET GRILLED WITH FRESH GOAT'S CHEESE, ROASTED PEPPERS AND RED PEPPER SAUCE

A colourful dish, but it needs last minute attention, so keep off the vino until the dish is 'en place'! The fillet steak tends to be the staple of restaurants but rump has good flavour and is my favourite for grilling. The fillet being round and compact works well for this dish.

Soften the chopped onion and garlic in the butter. Add the peppers and stock and simmer for 30 minutes. Blend to a smooth purée in a blender and pass through a fine sieve. Season and add cream or yogurt.

For the roasted peppers: Allow 1 pepper per person. De-seed and quarter. Place skin side up on a roasting tray and brush with olive oil. Roast in hot oven for 30 minutes after which skin should peel away. Toss with more oil, parsley and chives.

Grill or fry the steaks to taste. For medium rare about five minutes each side for thick steaks. Rest for ten minutes.

Place a slice of goat's cheese on each steak with seasoning, herbs and olive oil. Put under high grill until the cheese is browning.

Warm the sauce, place the peppers to one side and the steaks on top of the sauce.

For 8:

Eight 6-8oz (200g) fillet steaks

8oz (225g) fresh goat's cheese

1 tablespoon chopped

flat leaf parsley

1 tablespoon chopped chives

8 small red peppers

For the sauce:

4 red peppers, seeded

and chopped

½ pint chicken stock

(see Bare Necessities)

1 onion

2 cloves garlic

2oz (50g) butter

¼ pint cream or plain

thick yogurt

BAKER'S WINE SUGGESTION

This needs weight and interest too. Perhaps a really good Shiraz like Rockford or St Hallets Old Block. Otherwise go to Italy and try the excellent wine being made in the far south on the Salentino Penninsula from the Negroamaro grape. The best producer is Candido.

LAMB STEAKS BAKED 'EN AILLADE'

For 8:

8 steaks from the leg about
6oz (150g) each
3 onions
6 cloves garlic
8oz (225g) chopped tomatoes
¼ pint olive oil
½ bottle dry white wine
1 tablespoon fresh thyme (less
if using dried)
1 teaspoon dried oregano
8 sprigs of rosemary
seasoning
Rind and juice of four lemons
8oz (225g) breadcrumbs
Bunch of parsley chopped small

The leg of lamb that the English roast every Sunday and serve with vegetables and gravy is transformed in this dish into a succulent Provençal feast, full of the aroma of garlic, lemon and tomatoes.

The leg steaks can be marinated and lightly grilled, or barbecued, but may be a little tough for those used to fillet steaks and lamb chops. This dish braises the meat slowly and it just melts in the mouth.

Ask your butcher to cut the steaks about 1" thick with the bone left in.

In a sauté pan brown the steaks using half the olive oil, and put to one side. In the same pan and oil soften the finely chopped onion and half the garlic. Add the tomatoes and white wine, thyme and oregano, and seasoning and simmer for 20 minutes to make a rich sauce.

Meanwhile chop the remaining garlic, add to the breadcrumbs with the lemon rind and parsley.

Spread the sauce on the bottom of a generous gratin dish. Lay the steaks on the rosemary over the sauce, and cover with the breadcrumb mixture. Spoon the remaining olive oil and lemon juice over the top. Bake in a hot over (MK6 200C) for 45 minutes. Watch that the top does not burn and if the sauce looks too thick add a little water. Serve straight from the oven and remember just to remove the rosemary stalks as you serve the lamb. If you have decided to make your sauce the day before remember to cook the lamb for 15 minutes longer as the dish will be cold to start with.

PORK AND OFFAL

*T*his little piggy stayed at home – pork cookery, with the exception of charcuterie is really in the realm of home-cooking rather than that of the chef. The cuts of pork tend to require long roasting times and the inherent dryness of the meat can make it a risky choice for the restaurateur. At its best, pork is full of flavour, with that rich crackling and caramelised outside. Restaurants tend to use the fillet which is quick to cook but the bigger cuts have the flavour and the fat to enhance the longer cooking. Just because pork is unacceptable underdone, it does not need to be ruined. This especially applies to hams which really repay care being given to the cooking time to retain that moist middle.

We know all about pork and fruit, especially the apple, but the Italians use bags of garlic and rosemary cooking pork more in the way that we would think of for lamb. Their porchetta, the suckling pig boned and rolled with garlic and herbs gives off aromas that are the essence of Tuscany. The roast loin of pork recipe here is a reminder of Elizabeth David of the late sixties, while the pork with beetroot is Olive Tree chef Garry Rosser's entry into a 1996 chef competition. Timeless treatments.

You either like offal or you don't. Enthusiasts choose it when they can get it because they feel deprived much of the time. Calf's liver is a truly luxurious dish bearing little relation to the lamb's product. Very delicate and needs precious little cooking. Kidneys need careful trimming and again light cooking to avoid being rubbery.

We probably will see very little of sweetbreads, brains and the like in the future – what a shame for they are the preferred choice of a host of cooks! (A restaurant customer choosing Alsace or Rhône wine, eating offal and oysters is bound to be in the trade!)

I have included a sweetbread dish in the salads section simply because it's irresistibly delicious.

SAUTE OF CALF'S LIVER WITH LIME AND JUNIPERBERRIES

The first time I had calf's liver was in the late sixties at George Perry- Smith's extraordinary Hole In The Wall in Bath. Both the dish and the restaurant were a revelation. I seem to remember the sauce being of Dubonnet and orange, a very racey combination for the time. It is the extreme delicacy of the liver that is delectable if one's only memory is of perhaps overcooked lamb's liver.

First prepare the sauce by reducing the stock and wine, with the shallot and juniperberries, by half. Zest the limes, add the juice, honey and gin, with the softened butter swirled in to produce a smooth sauce.

Just before serving, lightly flour the liver, heat the clarified butter and fry the slices quickly for about 30 seconds each side. Serve on the sauce immediately, sprinkled with the lime zests and parsley.

For 8:
3lb (1.4K) liver carefully sliced
about ¼" thick.
2oz (50g) clarified butter
2oz (50g) flour
Chopped parsley

For the sauce:
½ pint veal stock
(see Bare Necessities)
¼ pint white wine
1 level tablespoon
crushed juniperberries
4 fresh limes
2 tablespoons honey
2oz (50g) soft butter
1 shallot finely chopped
4 tablespoons gin

BAKER'S WINE SUGGESTIONS

I'm tempted to suggest a large glass of very cold gin here but these are meant to be wine suggestions! You'll need something fairly strong to cope with the juniper. Go for a Carmignano Riserva from the Conte Contini Bonacossi in the rolling hills near Florence. A little known wine which deserves a better public.

FILLET OF PORK WITH BRAISED RED CABBAGE, APPLES AND SULTANAS

For 8:

4 trimmed pork fillets, sliced into
rounds, tapped out to make
'medaillons' 3" in diameter
2oz (50g) butter
2oz (50g) flour

For the cabbage:

1 large red cabbage, shredded
1 onion chopped
1 apple sliced
4oz(110g) sultanas
2oz (50g) soft brown sugar
4 tablespoons white wine vinegar
2oz (50g) butter
¼ pint chicken stock
(see Bare Necessities)
Salt and pepper

A winter dish with the great advantage that the cabbage can be cooked in advance, leaving only a few minutes of cooking for the pork. Care must be taken with the fillet, or tenderloin, as over-cooking could make the meat dry.

Soften the onion in the butter. Core and slice the apple, add to the onion with the cabbage and other ingredients. Stir together thoroughly and braise in a low oven for one hour. Do not let the cabbage dry out – add stock or water as necessary.

Just prior to serving, dust the pork in the flour and sauté in hot butter for a minute either side. Arrange decoratively on top of the cabbage.

BAKER'S WINE SUGGESTIONS

The red wines of the Loire sometimes suffer from the problem which besets the English winemaker – lack of sun to ripen the grapes. Some vignerons have consummate skill at producing red wines with good body and fruit – they even manage this sometimes, in poor years. One of the finest makes a Saumur Champigny from older vines. This is called Cuvée Lena Filliatreau. Well worth seeking out, its spicy but slightly tart flavours would go well with the cabbage and sultanas.

HOT WILTSHIRE HAM WITH APRICOTS AND MADEIRA

For a large party a whole, hot ham is a sumptuous alternative to beef or turkey at Christmas, with the glistening glaze and rich dark sauce somehow reminiscent of the Victorian kitchen.

The essentials are to cook the ham on the bone, with care over the cooking time, because judging by touch is that much harder than with a small cut of meat.

To prepare the uncooked ham, which may or may not be smoked depending on your preference, soak for at least 24 hours in cold water, changing the water two or three times.

Soak the dried apricots overnight.

To cook, cover with water, add peeled onion, bay leaves and pepper-corns and bring to the boil. Simmer for 15 minutes to the pound, removing any scum that may form. Allow to rest in the hot cooking liquid for a further 30 minutes. Remove onto a roasting tray. Carefully remove the skin and large areas of fat, but leave enough fat to act as a 'key' for the glaze. Coat the ham with the mixture and place in a preheated oven, very hot, for 15 to 20 minutes basting with more glaze as necessary to produce a slightly caramelised effect.

Simmer the apricots in the veal stock. Remove the apricots and reduce the stock by half. Add the madeira, redcurrant jelly, and season well. Whisk in 2oz softened butter and return apricots to the sauce.

Carve the joint by slicing downward to the knuckle bone. Serve with the very hot sauce.

For the glaze:

6 tablespoons honey

3 tablespoons coarse grain mustard

Salt, pepper and crushed juniperberries

For the sauce:

1lb (450g) dried apricots

½ pint veal stock

(see Bare Necessities)

Glass madeira

1 tablespoon redcurrant jelly

2oz (50g) butter

BAKER'S WINE SUGGESTIONS

 I would drink spicy white with this dish. Probably a very good Riesling like Hugel's Reserve Personnelle or Trimbach's Cuvée Frederick Emile. Both have a touch of richness which would help the apricots and Madeira and a lot of dryness in the finish for the ham.

CALVES KIDNEYS GRILLED, WITH WILD MUSHROOMS AND SPINACH

For 8 people you will need:

4 calves kidneys, halved, skinned and trimmed of all 'plumbing'
1lb (450g) fresh spinach
4oz (110g) wild mushrooms (girolles and chanterelles are good in the autumn, but dried porcini a good substitute and less extravagant)
½ pint veal stock
(see Bare Necessities)
Glass madeira
4oz (110g) butter.
Seasoning

Kidneys are not the first thing that women put in the shopping basket. They are popular in restaurants primarily with men, who if not the cuisinier at home, don't otherwise get many chances! The calves kidney however should not deter those who are slightly squeamish about offal, it is delicate in flavour and when properly prepared by the butcher quite straightforward to handle. The expense makes a little care worthwhile, and there are of course lamb's kidneys as a less extravagant alternative.

First, prepare a Madeira sauce by reducing the veal stock by half, adding the Madeira, and finishing with 1oz of soft butter and seasoning. Set aside.

Wash and de-stalk the spinach, slice the leaves, and cook on a high heat in butter for just long enough for the spinach to wilt.

Sauté the wild mushrooms in butter for two minutes (longer for dried mushrooms which must be washed and soaked carefully).

Grill the halved kidneys for about five minutes on each side so as to leave the kidney a little pink. Leave to rest for five minutes, then slice.

On individual plates make a bed of the piping hot spinach, spoon a little sauce into the centre and place the kidney and mushrooms on top.

BAKER'S WINE SUGGESTIONS

When I go to The Olive Tree this is one of my favourite dishes. As Claret is my preferred tipple it is this which I try to drink. It really is worth trying to afford something a little special so go for a classed growth from St Julien or Pauillac and try to find a wine from 1982, 1983 or 1985. These are still drinking superbly and will continue so to do for some years yet.

LOIN OF PORK ROASTED WITH GREMOLATA, PROVENCAL SAUCE

Much of the great meat cookery of France seems to revolve around the versatile pig – the cassoulets, charcuterie and daubes are synonymous with French country cooking. In England, we rarely go much beyond the Sunday joint of pork with apple sauce, apart from bacon which is often now of poor, watery quality. There is a degree of folklore about the need to cook pork for ever, but the loin is a delicious joint not requiring excessive cooking time, and great value for money!

Roast the pork for thirty minutes in a medium oven MK 5 (190C), remove and coat with gremolata. Replace in oven and roast for further 30 minutes. Rest for ten minutes before slicing.

For the sauce, soften the onion and garlic in olive oil. Add the remaining ingredients and cook for about 40 minutes until rich and shiny.

You will need for 8 people :
a piece of pork loin, off the bone with skin removed, leaving a thin layer of fat. The flank should be long enough just to allow the joint to be tied into a neat cylinder. No crackling on this dish!
Allow about 8oz (225g) per person

The gremolata forms a delicious herb and lemon crust:
8 tablespoons white breadcrumbs
4 tablespoons chopped parsley
2 cloves finely chopped garlic
Grated rind 4 lemons
Salt and pepper
Mix well together

For the Provencal sauce:
2 onions finely chopped
2 cloves garlic
3 tablespoons olive oil
½ bottle white wine
1 tablespoon mixed thyme, basil, oregano
½ pint chopped, skinned tomatoes (tinned usually have most flavour)
2 tablespoons tomato purée
2 tablespoons chopped parsley

BAKER'S WINE SUGGESTIONS

A strongly provençal dish here with lots of flavours. Provençal wines have improved by leaps and bounds in recent years. Most need bottle age, so look for older wines from Mas du Daumas Gassac or Domaine Trevallon

FILLET OF PORK WITH GRILLED BLACK PUDDING AND CUMIN SPICED BEETROOT

For 8:

4 pork fillets to allow 6oz (175g) per person, sliced into ¼" thick medaillons

1lb (450g) sliced black pudding

8 medium washed beetroot

1 pint red wine

½ pint red wine vinegar

2 level tablespoons brown sugar

Fresh thyme and flat parsley

2 cloves garlic

4 teaspoons ground cumin

½ pint veal stock

(see Bare Necessities)

Beetroot has never been associated with fine cooking. It must be that vinegary stuff we were all brought up on, that drowned the flavour of everything else, a bit like salad cream, the only food it went with was a baked potato! Prepared this way the root is delicate and sweet and a change from all those fruity combinations with pork.

To prepare beetroot, simmer whole beets with wine, wine vinegar, sugar, spices, and garlic until tender, about two hours depending on size of beetroot. Peel the beets.

Strain beetroot, sieving juice carefully and reduce to 1 pint. Add the veal stock and reduce by half for the sauce.

Sauté pork fillet in hot oil for five minutes and grill black pudding.

Dice the beetroot, toss with fresh herbs and arrange with the pork and black pudding, add the sauce.

A silk purse from a sow's rear?

BAKER'S WINE SUGGESTIONS

Whenever I eat Black Pudding I compare it to that served at the Côte St Jacques at Joingy a three star Michelin restaurant where the Lorrain Père et Fils are not frightened to put it on their great menu (they also serve it cold for breakfast). Here one drinks the local red wine, Irrancy and it is a perfect accompaniment. Irrancy is light Pinot Noir but I think a good Beaujolais Cru would also be delicious, preferably one of the meatier ones like Moulin à Vent, Brouilly or Morgon.

have often wondered why, on occasion, the dinner party cook will proffer a choice of puddings. An act of largesse that they would consider inappropriate for other courses, and a step sideways, in a way, to the commercial entreatments of the restaurant menu. Then I realised that this is a confidence thing. People understand puddings and can show off a bit. Guests understand puddings too and they know that chocolate and cream are chocolate and cream. Ask their view on the lamb or the wild duck and they will be more circumspect. Is a fishy wild duck a nice wild duck?

So pudding recipes I suggest with trepidation, to a knowledgeable audience. Many of the puddings served in my restaurants have been the work of colleagues in my kitchen and my thanks to them for their creative input.

We have loved the return to the traditional puddings of the past in that they are simple and honest to make and use sensible local materials. Unless you make a bread and butter pudding like Anton Mosimann, little can go wrong with these robust affairs. The elegant patisserie of haute cuisine can be demanding and extravagant, and I make no excuse for these contributions being homely and achievable.

Political culinary correctness seems to have left puddings largely unscathed, so go for them while you can!

BORDELAISE PEAR TART

Pears are something of a forgotten fruit these days, especially now that we have exotic fruits available all the year round. The best thing about them is that they lend themselves to cooking better than nearly any fruit, holding their shape and retaining their flavour.

Pears in red wine are a traditional treat and this tart is a variation on the theme.

Peel, core and quarter the pears and rub them immediately with lemon juice. Bring the wine, sugar and jelly to the boil and simmer with the pears until just soft. Remove the pears to a piece of kitchen paper and continue to reduce the wine by about half until just beginning to glaze. Butter the flan ring (one with a detachable base is simpler), and line with the shortcrust pastry. Chill for 30 minutes. Line the pastry with foil, fill with rice or beans and bake blind in a medium oven Mk4 (180C) for 15 minutes.

Remove the beans and add the cool pastry cream.

Lay the pears decoratively on the cream and glaze with the remaining wine mixture. The tart should be a deep glistening red.

You will need for one 10"
tart for 8 people:
8 conference pears
(best if a little under ripe)
½ bottle young claret
8oz (225g) caster sugar
2 tablespoons redcurrant jelly
½ pint pastry cream
(see Bare Necessities)
Rind and juice of 1 lemon
12oz (350g) sweet shortcrust
pastry (see Bare Necessities)
Beans or rice for blind baking

BAKER'S WINE SUGGESTION

 It must be a Bordeaux wine. Either go for one of the smaller, up and coming Châteaux of Sauternes like Bastor Lamontagne or Lamothe Guignard or look for a wine from a less well known part like Loupiac or Ste Croix du Mont – you may be well surprised by their quality.

For 8:

8 rounds of bread without crusts

1½ pints custard

(see Bare Necessities)

Rind and juice of 2 oranges

1 coffee cup dark rum

4oz (110g) butter

4oz (110g) soft brown sugar

4oz (110g) sultanas

Bread and butter pudding is fashionable restaurant fare these days, but really this is family food, because it works best when cooked in a generous dish, where the fun is having some of the crunchy top with some of the rich melted sauce at the bottom. Judge the cooking so that the custard is only just set.

This is a rather rich version with bags of flavour. We are in the business of 'fun' rather than fuel when it comes to recipes!

Choose a deep pudding dish. Butter the slices of bread and then layer with each layer having a sprinkling of the rum, sugar, orange rind and juice and sultanas.

Prepare the custard but do not cook it until thickened. Pour over the bread. You may need more or less custard depending on your dish, but it must come near the top.

Sprinkle remaining sugar on the top, bake at Mk 4 (180C) for 30 minutes or until just set. For a crunchy top finish under the grill. Serve with cream.

Delicious cold in the unlikely event of any being left over.

CARAMEL ICE CREAM

Use this basic method for all ice creams. The essential rules are that churning the ice cream by machine or by hand improves texture. Sugar and alcohol reduce the freezing point so the ice cream is softer. Never refreeze ice cream, but of course it is usually so good there is none left! Take great care with the very hot caramel.

For 8:
½ pint milk
6 egg yolks
Vanilla pod
12oz (350 g) sugar
1½ pints double cream

Make a custard with the eggs by heating ½ pint of milk and cream with the vanilla pod to just less than boiling and whisking on to the well beaten egg yolks.

Make caramel by carefully heating the sugar in a heavy bottomed pan large enough to accept the remaining cream.

Heat the cream and whisk into the caramel, add to the custard and thicken slowly, over low heat, stirring constantly.

Chill, churn and freeze.

BAKER'S WINE SUGGESTION

 A nice all round wine would be a Southern French Muscat from Frontignan or Riversaultes. These are darker in colour than the wines of Beaumes de Venise and tend to be a little more subtle and less cloying.

COLONIAL CRUMBLE

For 8:

1 Mango

1 Paw Paw

2 Kiwi fruit

2 Peaches

1 very small Pineapple

1 Banana.

¼ pint stock syrup

(see Bare Necessities)

For the topping:

6oz (175 g) plain flour

2oz (50g) ground almonds

4oz (110g) soft butter

4oz (110g) soft brown sugar

I have no doubt that the worthies of the British Raj never concocted any dish of tropical fruits such as this! We created this dish on a snowy January day when trying to think of how to make a good old winter pudding a bit more cheerful. This may not be like crumbles ought to be but it is a great winter dish.

Remember that the almond topping of the crumble is equally good with your regular apple and blackberry.

The fruits can be varied, the more colour the better.

Peel and slice the fruits into manageable spoon size bits, and poach in the stock syrup until tender, put in the bottom of a suitable crumble dish, with remaining syrup.

Mix the flour, almonds and sugar well and then rub in the butter with the fingertips. Cover the fruit with the topping and bake for 30-40 minutes until brown, Mk 4 (180C).

Serve with a crème fraîche or yogurt.

The boy will do the washing up, you may watch the polo.

BAKER'S WINE SUGGESTION

This exotic combination of fruit demands a wine with exotic flavours. For some years now the EC has forced a stop on the importation of sweet wines from the New World; that ban seems to have been removed and the deliciously ripe botrytised wines of South Africa and Australia are about again. The richest Australian I have encountered is the Noble One from de Bortoli; this is dressed to resemble Ch d'Yquem - it's not as good but is not as expensive either, about £10 per half. From South Africa there are many wonderful dessert wines: a particularly pleasing half is Delheim's Edelspatz, again plenty of raisiny fruit to compliment the exotic fruit and sweetness of the crumble.

WHISKY AND GINGER FLUMMERY WITH RHUBARB COMPOTE

One might think of this dish as a Scottish syllabub, rich and creamy but with a bit more 'attitude' than the the soft spoken lemon variety.

Add the sugar and the ginger to the cream, beat until just holding its shape. Add the whisky slowly, whipping continuously to form light but not scrambled whipped cream. For serving sprinkle the toasted oats on the top.

A higher octane version of this was, I think, called whim-wham where the cream included small almond macaroons soaked in whisky.

Serve with a compôte of rhubarb braised with sugar and a little orange juice.

For 8
½ pint double cream
Teaspoon finely chopped
fresh ginger
8 tablespoons whisky
4oz (110g) caster sugar
2 tablespoons toasted oats
1lb rhubarb
¼ pint orange juice

BAKER'S WINE SUGGESTION

The whisky flavour does not dominate here. Go for something really unusual. In the Province of Verona a talented wine maker called Macaulan is making the best sweet wine that Italy has yet seen. It is called Torcolato. Rather expensive (guide price £20) but well worth the experiment.

HOT CHOCOLATE SOUFFLE

For 8 soufflés:

18oz (500g) dark chocolate

2oz (50g) butter

1 coffeecup rum

9 egg yolks

13 fl oz egg whites

A slightly jaded member of staff, when asked, for the umpteenth time, by a customer what an hot chocolate soufflé was, replied "its a soufflé, its made of chocolate and its hot!" what more can you say

This recipe is designed to be cooked in individual dishes and is less successful when cooked in a large quantity, as it is a flour-free soufflé.

In a double saucepan, melt the chocolate and butter. Remove from the heat, gently stir in the rum and egg yolks.

Whisk the whites until just holding their shape, then stir in one third of the whites into the chocolate mixture, followed by the remainder carefully folded in.

Lightly butter the dishes, dust with flour, and fill to 1" from the top. Bake in a preheated oven Mk6 (200C) for 15 minutes. The soufflé should be just runny in the centre.

Offer cream or a little warm vanilla custard (see Bare Necessities) to pour into the centre.

BAKER'S WINE SUGGESTION

This is very rich stuff – in addition to anything else you'll need some cold fizzy water. As everyone knows its almost impossible to match wine with chocolate. There is a strange wine called Essencia from California made with the Orange Muscat grape. This really does have an orange flavour so a swig of this and a spoon of the soufflé makes a highly superior Terrys Chocolate Orange. I think I'd stick with the water!

LIGHT AND DARK CHOCOLATE PARFAIT WITH COFFEE BEAN SAUCE

The word parfait seems to be applied on menus these days to every kind of smooth firm dish from chicken livers to fish. Correctly it is an ice cream type mixture where the custard is not cooked. This is a showy dinner party dish, rich but elegant with a penalty of rather too many bowls to wash up afterwards!

In two separate bowls, over hot water melt the two different chocolates.

In separate bowls, whisk 2 eggs and 2 yolks in each bowl, until thick but light (ribbon stage). Mix into each chocolate mixture.

Lightly whip the cream and fold half into each batch of chocolate.

Line the terrine or mould with cling film, and pour in a layer of one colour. Set in the freezer, add next layer and so on until all the mixtures are used. A looser artistic interpretation is to swirl the two mixtures together to get a marbled effect. Each to his/her own!

Coffee bean sauce.

Lightly grind 2 tablespoons coffee beans.

Make 1 pint custard (see Bare Necessities) by adding the coffee beans to the milk as it is being heated to make the custard, and chill well to serve under the parfait.

For an eight portion 'terrine' of parfait you will need:
7oz (200g) bitter dark chocolate
7oz (200g) white chocolate
4 whole eggs
4 yolks
1 pint double cream

Coffee bean sauce:
2 tablespoons coffee beans
1 pint custard (see Bare Necessities)

BAKER'S WINE SUGGESTION

The same problem here as with the Soufflé. I think a very large espresso would be the thing here or for the less wary an Irish coffee!

ORANGE AND CARDAMOM TART

For a deep 10" flan case:

2 pints fresh orange juice

About 12 crushed cardamom seeds (the little black bits)

9 eggs

14oz (400g) caster sugar

½ pint half whipped double cream

Juice and zest of 4 oranges

14oz (400g) sweet shortcrust pastry (see Bare Necessities)

Bake blind using foil or beans

I think that I first had this combination as an ice cream and it may have been at Joyce Molyneaux's wonderful Carved Angel at Dartmouth. We of course immediately borrowed the idea and then moved on to using this sweet spicey taste as a change to the ubiquitous lemon tart.

There is some care to be taken with the cooking; keep it slow and low to avoid the filling separating, and cover with foil if the top is looking too coloured.

Reduce the orange juice with the cardamom by half.

Whisk the eggs and sugar until thick enough to hold their shape, the 'ribbon' stage. Add the strained juice with the zests of the oranges. Fold in the cream.

Pour into the flan case and bake at Gas Mk 1/2 (130C) for 1 ½ hours until set.

Delicious served with a Grand Marnier ice cream (See ice cream recipe pg 115).

BAKER'S WINE SUGGESTION

Strong flavours like this are difficult. Some people love a wine called Orange Muscat and Flora made by the huge Australian firm of Brown Brothers. If you like really sweet orangey goo then this is for you. Alternatively go for a late harvest Loire wine from the Chenin Blanc grape. Something with a bit of age from Huet in Vouvray would be splendid. Alternatively look for anything from a good vintage from Bonnezeaux or Quarts de Chaume. The recent 1989/90 super duo from the Loire are so ripe that they can be enjoyed now but will of course benefit from keeping well into the next century.

PRUNE AND ARMAGNAC TART

There are certain flavours which are completely complementary. Perhaps because the finest prunes originate from the same area as Armagnac we have become accustomed to their marriage, but for whatever reason this is a classic combination.

To make the filling, beat the butter until soft. Mix the sugar and ground almonds and add to the soft butter. Then work in the flour and add the eggs one by one, beating until light. Finally add the rum.

Preheat the oven to Gas Mk 4 (180C).

Roll out the pastry as thinly as you dare and line a 10" flan ring with removable base (or individual rings). Spread half the filling over the base of the tart, add a layer of well-drained prunes saving the juice for later, then cover with the remainder of the filling.

Bake in the oven for 30 minutes (individual tarts 15 to 20 minutes). After 10 minutes lower the oven temperature to Gas Mk 2 (150C) and cover, if the centre of the tart is not completely set.

Cool slightly then turn out of the flan case.

Serve with flavoured double cream. This is made by whipping a half pint double cream with a little sugar and armagnac to taste from the prune marinade.

For 8:

12 oz (350g) sweet shortcrust pastry

8oz (225g) Agen or Californian prunes which have been macerated in Armagnac for at least 48 hours

For the filling:

4oz (110g) unsalted butter

4oz (110g) icing sugar

4oz (110g) ground almonds

2oz (50g) plain flour

3 eggs

2 tablespoons dark rum

BAKER'S WINE SUGGESTION

 Try a small glass or Vielle Prune a marvellous Eau de Vie made in the Armagnac area. It is matured for a year or two in old Armagnac casks. Alternatively a good Muscat from the South of France or Beaumes de Venise. This is now a bit of a cliché and many find them obvious and too sweet. If you go for a good one like that of the Domaine de Durban and chill it well it is an excellent light dessert wine.

REDCURRANT SORBET

For eight generous portions:
2lbs (900g) redcurrants
Rind and juice of one orange
4oz (110g) sugar (excluding syrup)

For a sugar syrup:
Boil 4oz (110g) sugar with
½ pint of water until forming a
light syrup

This recipe for a fruit sorbet can act as a 'master' for all varieties of fruit sorbets. The principle is the use of a sugar syrup to create the softness of the texture, the more sugar the softer the sorbet will be. Likewise with the addition of alcohol.

The variety of machines on the market make home-made sorbets straightforward, although there was an occasion early in my career when a colleague even less experienced than me, when asked to add the salt to the sorbet machine added it to the sorbet not to the ice that surrounded the sorbet! Astonishingly the guests were a group of Trust House managers who ate the sorbet and never said a thing, so I expect that at all of their hotels salt was added to the sorbets because that's how it was done at the famous Thornbury Castle!

Stirring the mixture in a metal bowl occasionally as it freezes is still a low tech method that works.

Bring the fruit and sugar gently to the boil with no water and remove from the heat. Blend in a liquidiser and pass through a fine sieve. Chill. Combine the syrup and purée together. You may not want too sweet a mixture, therefore add less syrup. If you have an ice cream machine churn the sorbet until set. Otherwise place the mixture in the freezer and beat occasionally during the freezing process to prevent ice crystals.

Leaving some whole redcurrants in the mixture makes for interest if one doesn't mind the bits!

BAKER'S WINE SUGGESTION

A bit of fizz goes well with sorbet – try a Fraise de Bois from Gabriel Boudier topped up with champagne, very well chilled.

STEAMED HOT CHOCOLATE PUDDING

The love affair of the British with chocolate combines here with the traditionalism of a proper old-fashioned steamed pud. A winter dish, and custard (see Bare Necessities) is a very good alternative to the chocolate sauce. The dish is designed for cooking in individual moulds or ramekins, but will work well enough in a large pudding basin with an extra allowance for cooking time.

Cream butter and sugar. Blend in the cocoa and ground almonds. Add the egg yolks one at a time. Whisk the egg whites. Mix in a third of the whites and carefully fold in the rest. Add the grated chocolate.

Butter the pudding moulds carefully, divide the mixture between them, cover with greaseproof paper.

Steam in a bain-marie for 35 minutes gas Mk 4 (180C).

For the chocolate sauce, melt chocolate and sugar in the water in a basin over water until smooth and syrupy. Whisk in an egg yolk for a thicker sauce.

For eight individual puddings
(3 pints):
4oz (110g) grated dark chocolate
4oz (110g) butter
4oz (110g) caster sugar
1oz (25g) cocoa powder
3oz (75g) ground almonds
6 eggs separated

Chocolate sauce:
6oz (175g) bitter chocolate
4oz (110g) caster sugar
(vanilla flavoured or add a few drops of essence)
1 pint water
1 egg yolk optional

BAKER'S WINE SUGGESTION

Philip Togni is a part English part Swiss who has been making wine in the Napa Valley since the nineteen fifties. His most interesting wine is called Ca' Togni and it is from the Black Hamburg grape. This grape makes dessert wine with enormous bouquet and with a flavour and weight somewhat like a tawny port. It is a good match with chocolate. If you are French or think the French know everything there is to know about food and wine then allow the sommelier to suggest a Banyuls which is what they think goes well with Chocolate .... I am not so sure.

For eight individual jelly moulds:

½ bottle sweet Muscat such as Beaumes de Venise

12oz (350g) caster sugar

6 leaves gelatine, softened in enough cold water to immerse the leaves. The water is discarded

2lb (900g) soft fruit

NB Gelatine. The 'trade' uses leaf gelatine which is very much easier to use. Equivalent to 6 leaves would be 2½oz sachets of dried powder, dissolved in some of the wine and then warmed

We must all be children at heart if the success of jellies in the restaurant is anything to go by. Raspberry and claret or champagne they are all popular – but maybe the alcohol has something to do with it!

The summer fruits can be made up of all sorts of combinations, the main appeal being colours and textures, but prepare them in small pieces.

Prepare a total of about 2lb (900g) of soft fruits neatly chopped in irregular shapes keeping some whole berries such as blueberries or raspberries.

Dissolve the sugar in the warmed wine, but avoid boiling. Add the softened gelatine. Put some of the jelly in the moulds with some of the fruit, chill to set, add more jelly and fruit and repeat the process until all is used. The short-cut of filling the moulds in one go results in all the fruit sinking to the bottom!

Chill overnight. To serve, gently warm the moulds and turn out. A raspberry sauce is a delicious and pretty accompaniment.

BAKER'S WINE SUGGESTION

This deliciously light jelly should be made with the best Muscat de Beaumes de Venise that is produced. This comes from Jacques Leydier and is called Domaine de Durban. It is somewhat more expensive than most wines from the village but it is altogether superior, although light in colour it packs a real punch as far as flavour is concerned. Do not settle for a second best in this case.

SUMMER PUDDING

The idea of summer pudding is to make use of those fruits that are ready together as the season progresses, so there is no place for a fixed recipe. The red berries are essential for the rich colour but gooseberries work well and some add apple.

Prepare the fruits, but don't be obsessive about every berry stalk. Allow 4oz (110g) fruit per person, 2lb (900g) mixed fruits for 8 people.

For 8 people:
1 stale white sliced loaf
2lb (900g) mixed fruit
8oz (225g) caster sugar

Bring the fruit gently to the boil with 8oz (225g) sugar, less if you prefer a tart pudding. Do not add water. Remove from the heat and strain off the liquid, perhaps more than once. Allow to cool.

Remove the crust from stale white bread, slice and cut into wedges suitable for lining a pudding basin. Use individual moulds or a larger one. The larger the pudding the greater the challenge when one turns it out! Soak the bread thoroughly in the fruit juices, and line the basin.

Spoon in the fruit pressing down well, and cover when full with more soaked bread.

Weight the top and chill for at least 24 hours.

Turn out the pudding and serve the remaining juices separately or poured over the top.

BAKER'S WINE SUGGESTION

The place for a great Sauternes like Climens, Suduiraut and their cousins. These are at last starting to gain in popularity (quite rightly they are superbly made wines) and thus in price (unfortunate but inevitable). 1983s are drinkable now but for value go to 1981. Earlier and more expensive vintages to look for are 1976, 1975 and 1971.

For 8:

*About 24 ripe figs depending
on size*

*Good wine glass of grappa
or schnapps*

4oz(110g) butter

8oz(225g) soft brown sugar

12 limes

This is the light healthy pudding that people say they want, but the grappa gives it the touch of decadence that figs somehow seem to need.

The figs need to be beautifully ripe as the cooking is for a few minutes only.

For the sorbet, see redcurrant sorbet (p122) and substitute the rind and juice of 12 limes for the redcurrants. Do not cook the limes with sugar, otherwise proceed as indicated

Prepare the figs by slicing a cross on the top of each fig, to form petal shapes and liberally marinade the fruit with the grappa. Leave to stand for 30 minutes.

When ready to serve, place a small dot of softened butter on each fig, sprinkle with sugar and grill under a hot grill for about 5 minutes, to dissolve the sugar but avoid leaving too long or the figs may collapse.

Serve immediately with the sorbet on the side and perhaps an ice-cold glass of grappa.

NIBBLES

We sometimes in a restaurant kitchen are desperate to change something that we have been doing for ages because we are fed up with it. The problem is that your guests don't see it that way, and if a familiar friend on the menu is missing they will say "but where is your so and so, that's why we come"

This certainly applies to our fish soup which I dare not take off the menu, the gratin dauphinois, and certainly to these two little nibbles.

OLIVE TREE CHEESE AND ANCHOVY PASTRIES

For eight people:
8oz (225g) puff pastry
Small tin of anchovy fillets
6oz (175g) grated
mature cheddar
Pepper
1 egg

Roll out the pastry into a long sheet about ¼" thick, 6" wide.

Spread the cheese all over, season.

Lay the anchovies in two lines one end to the other, as a railway line. Fold the pastry edges over the anchovy so that they form a join down the centre.

Brush with beaten egg and fold over again to form a swiss roll. Chill. Slice carefully into ¼" slices and lay flat on a baking sheet, leaving space for the pastries to expand.

Bake Mk 6 (200C) for 15 minutes.

Watch out, the most common aroma from the Olive Tree kitchen at 6.00pm is of burned "cheesies"!

MUSSELS WITH WATERCRESS BUTTER

For nibbles for 8 people you are going to need about 4 dozen mussels, perhaps 2lb(1k)

8oz (225g) bunch watercress

8oz(225g) butter

8oz(225g) breadcrumbs

1 clove finely chopped garlic

Salt and pepper

For a Valentine's night dinner party you might be a little more risqué and try this with oysters. With cooked mussels avoid leaving under the grill for long or you get india rubber nibbles

Prepare mussels in the usual way (see p 48) or buy cooked mussels

Soften the garlic in the butter. Remove the thick part of the cress stems, roughly chop the remainder and just wilt in the garlic butter. Blend in a liquidiser until smooth. Season well. Add the crumbs to make a stiff paste. Spoon over the mussels and place under a hot grill to brown.

FILO MONEY BAGS

For a dozen bite size filos

8oz (225g) filo pastry

2oz (50g) melted butter

1 onion

2oz (50g) butter

4oz (110g) mushrooms

4oz (110g) breadcrumbs

coffeespoon each of ground Cumin, coriander, cardamom seeds

Salt and pepper

Little filo money bags started to appear in the eighties in restaurants as first courses, main courses, vegetables and even puddings, but really they are an ideal nibble, to put one's money bag where one's mouth...

Soften the onion and mushroom in the butter with the spices, add the breadcrumbs to stiffen the mixture. Cool.

Cut the filo into 4" squares. Buttering each sheet lay four sheets one on top of the other, placing each sheet at 45 degrees to the previous, forming an asterisk pattern.

Spoon mixture into the middle, crimp the neck of the bag with fingers and fold back the folds of the bag. Brush with melted butter.

Bake in hot oven Mk6 200C for about five minutes. Serve very hot.

QUICK CHOCOLATE TRUFFLES

To make 50 small truffles:

½ pint whipping cream

10oz (250g) bitter plain chocolate

4 tablespoons rum

8oz (225g) cocoa powder

Nobody wants to eat them but everyone does! This is a quick method for truffles which can be made to look a little more professional by dipping in melted chocolate to form a casing.

Break the chocolate into pieces and add the rum in a bowl placed over hot water and melt the chocolate slowly.

Heat the cream and pour onto the chocolate, whisk thoroughly.

Use a piping bag to pipe the truffles onto a tray lined with silicone paper. Chill. Roll in the cocoa powder and keep in the fridge.

OLIVE TREE CHOCOLATE FUDGE

1lb 4oz (550g) caster sugar

4oz (110g) glucose

1½ pints double cream

8oz (225g) bitter chocolate

8oz (225g) melted butter

This will be enough for a few days after the dinner party for eight! It has the highest concentration of calories by volume known to man.

In a large pan that will allow the fudge to rise as it boils, bring all the ingredients to the boil stirring occasionally, and cook until 'softball' stage is reached, 120C if you have a sugar thermometer. To test, drop a spoonful into cold water where it should set into a soft ball. Mind your fingers!

Allow to cool stirring frequently. When just beginning to set, pour into an oiled baking tray. When still soft but firm cut into squares. Turn out when set.

This is a soft fudge and should be kept in the fridge, preferably with a padlock.

Artichoke and crab salad | 37

Asparagus and wild mushroom salad | 33

Aubergine, mozzarella and parma ham fritters | 57

Aubergine, tomato and field mushroom salad | 34

Avgolemono | 25

Béarnaise sauce | 18

Beef
fillet with fresh goat's cheese | 101
rump with armagnac and muscat grapes | 97
skirt braised with elderberry vinegar | 95

Beetroot, cumin spiced | 110

Bordelaise pear tart | 113

Bread
brioche | 22
rolls, white and brown | 12

Calves
kidneys with wild mushrooms and spinach | 108
liver with lime and juniperberries | 105

Caramel ice cream | 115

Ceviche of turbot and limes | 45

Cheese and anchovy pastries | 128

Cheese beignets | 58

Chicken
breast with lemon. garlic, mint and yoghurt | 88
coq au vin | 81
liver tart | 59
salad of marinated chicken breast | 35
stock | 13
with apple and calvados | 87

Chocolate
fudge | 130
parfait with coffee bean sauce | 119
sauce | 123
soufflé | 118
steamed pudding | 123
truffles | 130

Cod
roast with pinenut crust | 77

Colonial crumble | 116

Crab
and artichoke salad and fresh limes | 37
saffron crab in watercress pancakes | 54
soup with cumin and coriander | 26

Crème patissiere | 21

Custard | 21

Dressing
hot chilli | 16
mayonnaise | 17
salsa verde | 16
vinaigrette | 15
yoghurt and coriander | 16
yoghurt and mint | 34

Duck
and plum terrine | 60
with lentils, bacon and garlic | 85

Elderberry vinegar | 95

Figs with grappa | 126

Filo money bags | 129

Fish
cakes, smokey with lemon and dill | 52
stock | 14

Fudge, chocolate | 130

Gnocchi with saffron courgettes | 62

Goat's cheese
fresh herb salad | 42
with beef fillet | 101
hazelnut tart | 61

Gratin dauphinois | 82

Grey mullet, braised oriental | 71

Grouse
roast with port and cranberries | 92

Guinea fowl
breast in pastry with lime and orange | 86

Hake baked with cheese and cider | 72

Ham with apricots and madeira | 107

Hare, roast saddle with wild mushrooms | 89

Hollandaise sauce | 18

Hot chocolate soufflé | 118

Ice cream
caramel | 115

John Dory steamed in spinach | 73

Kidneys, Calves with wild mushrooms | 108

Lamb
'en aillade' | 102
leg braised in red wine, oranges and rosemary | 99
rack with mint crust | 96
shoulder with cinnamon and cloves | 98

Leek and chive soup | 28

Lemon and dill cream | 52

Lemon pearl barley | 77

Lemon sole with crab and watercress | 74

Lime sorbet | 126

Liver, calves with lime & juniper berries | 105

Mackerel
with piquant raspberry sauce | 75

Mayonnaise | 17

Monkfish
and bacon salad | 36
spiced with saffron rice | 78

Mussels
with watercress butter | 129
with fresh pasta | 46

Orange and cardamom tart | 120

Osso buco | 100

Pancakes
watercress with saffron crab | 54

Pasta, fresh spinach with scallops, prawns and mussels | 46

Pastry
brioche | 22
choux | 58
cream | 21
puff | 20
shortcrust | 19
sweet shortcrust | 19

Pears, bordelaise pear tart | 113

Peppers
red pepper sauce | 101
roasted | 101

Pheasant
    pot-roasted with savoy cabbage   84
    and bacon

Pigeon
    breast and avocado salad   41
    roast with garlic cream sauce   90

Pork
    fillet braised with red cabbage   106
    and apples
    fillet with black pudding and   110
    cumin spiced beetroot
    loin roasted with gremolata   109

Potatoes, gratin dauphinois   82

Pot-au-feu of red mullet and crayfish   47

Prawn and anchovy mayonnaise   51

Quails' eggs, leek and saffron tart   65

Provençal fish soup   27

Prune and armagnac tart   121

Rabbit blanquette   82

Red mullet
    pot-au-feu   47
    with orange and rosemary   76

Red onion compôte   91

Redcurrant sorbet   122

Relishes   16

Rhubarb compôte   117

Risotto of seafood   48

Roast mediterranean vegetables   63

Roe deer, roast haunch with red onions   91

Rolls
    Olive Tree soft white   12
    Olive Tree brown   12

Roquefort and walnut soufflé   64

Rum and orange bread and   114
butter pudding

Saffron courgettes   62

Saffron rice   78

Salad of
    artichoke, crab and fresh lime   37
    asparagus and wild mushroom   33
    aubergine, tomato and field mushroom   34
    marinated chicken breast   35
    monkfish and bacon   36
    pigeon breast, avocado and radicchio   41
    Niçoise   38
    scallops and squid   39
    warm fresh goat's cheese   42
    warm spiced sweetbreads with girolles   40
    wild mushroom and asparagus   33

Salmon
    coulibiac   70
    seared fillet with prawn and anchovy   51
    mayonnaise

Salsa verde   16

Sauce
    chocolate   123
    coffee bean   119
    cumberland   60
    garlic cream   90
    hollandaise   18
    lemon and dill   52
    lime and orange   86
    orange and rosemary butter   76
    port and cranberry   92
    provencal   109
    raspberry   75
    red pepper   101
    rouille   27
    shallot and mint   96
    sorrel hollandaise   69
    sweet pepper and tomato   58
    watercress   74

Scallop
    and squid salad   39
    tart   49
    with fresh pasta   46

Seabass
    with fennel and tomato   69

Seafood bruschetta   50

Seafood risotto   48

Smokie fishcakes with lemon   52
and dill cream

Sorbet
    lime   126
    redcurrant   122

Soufflé
    hot chocolate   118
    roquefort and walnut   64

Soup
    avgolemono   25
    cornish crab with cumin and coriander   26
    leek and chive   28
    provençal fish   27
    spiced parsnip   29
    tourrin bourdelais   30

Spiced monkfish with saffron rice   78

Spiced parsnip soup   29

Squid and scallop salad   39

Stocks
    chicken   13
    fish   14
    veal   14

Sugar syrup   19

Summer fruit and muscat jelly   124

Summer pudding   125

Sweetbread and girolle salad   40

Sweet and sour leeks   66

Tart
    bordelaise pear   113
    orange and cardamom   120
    prune and armagnac   12
    quails eggs with leeks and saffron   65

Tourrin bordelais   30

Tuna carpaccio   53

Turbot ceviche   45

Vanilla custard   21

Veal
    shin braised with tomatoes   100
    stock   14

Venison
    and juniper rissoles   66
    roast haunch   91

Watercress pancakes with saffron crab   54

Watercress sauce   74

Whisky and ginger flummery   117

Wild mushroom and asparagus salad   33

Many of the wines suggested by Bill Baker with the recipes may be purchased from the following suppliers:

All areas, with emphasis on fine Burgundy and claret:

Reid Wines
The Mill
Marsh Lane
Hallatrow
Bristol BS18 5EB
(01761) 452645

Rhône and Loire specialists:

Yapp Brothers Ltd
Mere
Wiltshire BA12 6DY
(01747) 860423

Burgundy specialists, plus new world:

Domaine Direct
29 Wilmington Square
London WC1X 0EG
(0171) 8371142

All regions:

Christopher Piper Wine Ltd
1 Silver Street
Ottery St Mary
Devon EX11 1DB
(01404) 814139

Great Western Wine Co Ltd
The Wine Warehouse
Wells Road
Bath BA2 3AP
(01225) 446009

NOTES

NOTES

While I think that the degree of precision required is largely
a question of the individual temperament of each cook,
I would also remind readers that reliance on precise recipes
alone can be a trap. Marcel Boulestin wrote:

*'The dangerous person in the kitchen is the
one who goes rigidly by weights, measurements,
thermometers and scales'*

ELIZABETH DAVID ITALIAN FOOD 1954